THE COMPLETE MEAL PREP INSTANT POT COOKBOOK

Delicious, Simple, and Quick Meal Prep Recipes for Your Instant Pot

Disclaimer

I want your life to be as full of delicious and nutritious food as possible. But I also want you to be out there, enjoying your awesome life, instead of spending your whole life chained to the stove.

That's why I've created this brilliant *Meal Prep Instant Pot book*. You can slash the time you spend cooking, yet still feed your body exactly what it needs to thrive.

But please remember, I'm not a medical professional, nor a professional chef nor am I qualified to advise you on the kind of food you should (or shouldn't) be eating. Therefore, please consult a medical professional before you make any changes to your diet or lifestyle. Hopefully, you'll already be eating a wholefood diet and so are already pretty healthy, but it's always a good idea to check anyway. By eating the food in this cookbook, you do so at your own risk and assume all associated risk involved.

No responsibility is taken for any loss or damage related directly or indirectly to the information in this book. Never disregard professional medical advice or delay in seeking it because of something you have read in this book or in any linked materials.

Table of Contents

Introduction

Are you ready to transform the way you eat?

Okay, okay...I know what you're thinking.

You're thinking that this is one of those crazy diet/fitness/exercise books that lays down ridiculous claims at the beginning of the book, so it can hook you right in and 'convert' you to their way of eating.

You're right to be cynical. I would be too.

But this isn't one of your usual fad diet cookbooks. In fact, this book has *nothing* to do with fad diets, the latest trend or strange eating habits at all.

It's about making your eating habits easier, slashing the time you need to spend in the kitchen, and if you want, making the food that crosses your lips as healthy as possible.

And all of this will be done without making compromises, sacrifices or avoiding whole food groups (although you can do this too, if you chose to.)

Your first secret weapon will be meal prep.

Your second secret weapon will be your Instant Pot.

Nothing more, nothing less.

Yes, it really is that simple.

What to expect in this book

Through the pages of this book, I'll be guiding you through the whole meal prep process, from organizing yourself, getting everything ready and the actual cooking process.

I'll explain what meal prep is and how it can transform the way that you eat. I'll also explain how to get started without feeling overwhelmed. Then I'll explain why your Instant Pot will take your meal prep to the next level, and how you can use it to create awesome meals.

Finally, I'll share plenty of inspiring meal prep recipes that cover all your meals, from breakfast, lunch and dinner and are suitable for all kinds of diets, including vegan and vegetarian, Paleo, Keto, dairy-free, grain-free, gluten-free and more.

You'll have full instructions on how to cook these meals in your Instant Pot and eat amazing food in less time than you ever thought possible.

I'll also be sharing plenty of tips along the way that will help you hack your meal prep and learn how to use your Instant Pot if you're a newbie with either of these.

You just need your kitchen, a meal prep plan and some groceries and you can start meal prepping right away. It's that easy!

So, if you're ready to master the 'art' of meal prep, let's get started!

PART I: Meal Prep and the Instant Pot 101

Chapter 1: What is Meal Prep?

Let's start at the most important part of all, by talking about what meal prep is.

The name is actually 'meal preparation', and as you might expect from the name, it involves preparing your meals before you want to eat them.

This might mean that you choose to meal prep your breakfast, so you can actually eat a decent breakfast before you rush out of the door.

Or you might find yourself spending far too much money on takeaway sandwiches at work so decide to prep your lunches.

Or maybe you arrive home late, or tired and don't have the energy to get preparing your meals. You might even decide to dive in and start meal prepping all your meals for the week, so you have one less thing to worry about.

All you have to do when it's time to each is reach for the food you've already prepared, perhaps quickly reheat if needed, and you have a delicious and nutritious meal waiting for you.

As you can imagine, it's perfect if you have a busy life, if you want to streamline your habits, if you have new projects you want to launch (side hustle perhaps?) or you'd just prefer not to waste all that time in the kitchen! It's also a great way of sticking to your healthy eating habits and resisting the often-irresistible call of temptation that can often strike when you're hungry and unprepared.

Why Meal Prep using an Instant Pot?

Using an Instant Pot to help you meal prep will make the whole process so much easier. It will help you multitask much more easily, it will slash the time you need to spend on that dish and you'll have much less to wash up compared with other cooking methods.

Depending on the size of your Instant Pot, you should be able to cook much larger quantities of food, therefore providing you with plenty to last you the entire week.

Of course, you absolutely *can* meal prep without an Instant Pot, but it won't be nearly as much fun.

See? I told you that this stuff was easy! And it's also a brilliant way to streamline your life.

But these aren't the only benefits of meal prep...turn to the next chapter to find out what else it can do for your life and eating habits...

Chapter 2: What are the Benefits of Meal Prep?

I won't insult your intelligence by reminding you that the main benefit of meal prep is to save time in the kitchen. That's why you downloaded this book. You want an easier life and you don't want to compromise when it comes to eating great food. Just a couple of hours in the kitchen and you're done, right?

But did you know that meal prep has a ton of other benefits which will transform your life? Let me tell you more about them!

#1. You'll save money

When you meal prep, you're able to get much more organised and buy exactly what you need every time.

There will be no more last-minute trips to the supermarket, no more buying unnecessary treats or other items that just lie there in your pantry.

And you can also buy in bulk, or opt for more nutritious, lower-priced items which you might otherwise avoid because they take far too much time and hassle to cook. The Instant Pot removes this problem by cooking your food fast and efficiently.

You'll also save a ton of money on lunch when you do meal prep (have you ever added those things up??) and instead be able to start investing in your savings instead. Or splashing out on stuff that you love....

#2. You'll get healthier

There's no need to resist temptation or battle a hungry stomach when all the food on offer is a candy bar or bag of potato chips.

You'll always have the most nutritious food with you, it will (hopefully) be as nutritionally balanced as possible, and thanks to your Instant Pot, it should be absolutely bursting with vitamins, minerals, healthy protein, healthy fats and a ton of other good stuff.

#3. You'll lose weight

Meal prep effortlessly teaches you the art of portion control, which will make a massive difference in any quest you're on to lose weight. As mentioned above, you'll also be able to make healthier food choices, watch your calorie intake, and track your macros which will have a positive impact upon your waistline.

#4. You'll reduce food waste

When you're such a Zen master at meal prep, you'll stop wasting food that went bad before you got chance to eat it because you'll only need to buy exactly what you need. Which will, of course, save you money and save the planet too. Awesome bonus!

#5. You'll save time (and effort) in the supermarket

I was astonished at how much time I was saving grocery shopping when I started to food prep. Instead of wandering around, confused about what I wanted to buy and making it all up on the spot, I had a plan of attack! I had my list, I had my pen, and I just did it!

#6. You'll reduce your stress levels

Let's be honest- thinking about food can be stressful. Especially when you have a deadline at work, you have a crazy-busy lifestyle, or you have other commitments that drain your time. You just want it to be easy. Meal prep takes all this the pressure off. You don't have to puzzle about what to have for dinner or rush around, just follow the plan.

#7. You'll keep your meals varied

When you're stressed out and stuck for ideas on what to cook, it's all too easy to get trapped eating the same repetitive meals again and again. Meal prep makes this all much easier. Because you can think through your meals ahead of time, you can make sure you're eating foods from all the different food groups and switch them to your heart's content. Brilliant!

#8. You'll discover a new love of food!

When I started doing meal prep, it was simply to save time in the kitchen. I didn't have the time nor the inclination to do much more. But after a while, I found myself searching new recipes online, feeling inspired about food again, feeling energized and optimistic at the healthy food choices that could be out there, and having a fab time. The same thing could happen to you!

Are you convinced yet about meal prep and the Instant Pot? You should be!

So, let's not hang around- I want to talk to you about how to do meal prep. Find out how in the next chapter...

Chapter 3: How to 'Properly' Meal Prep

Let's get one thing straight right from the word *'Go'*...There ISN'T a 'proper' way to meal prep.

Anyone who tells you otherwise is clearly one of those crazy perfectionist types who has far too much time on their hands or doesn't have much of a social life!

The truth is, everyone has their own way to meal prep. Through actually doing meal prep for a while and tweaking how you do it, you'll find the most effective way for you and your lifestyle.

That being said, there are a few tips I'd like to share with you on how you can really make this work for you.

#1: Pick the best day

Before you do anything else, pick the day (or days) you'll be doing the meal prep.

Most people like to choose Sundays because it's the day when there are fewer interruptions, less obligations and you're likely to have more time on your hands. And if you need extra help in the kitchen, there will probably be someone around who can lend you a hand.

But a word of warning- don't try to take on too much at once. Start by prepping your meals for three or four days and see how it goes. This gentle start will make sure the whole meal prep process is a lot of fun and you'll learn as you go without ever feeling overwhelmed.

#2: Grab a calendar

Next, you'll need a large calendar or a piece of paper where you can visually outline your meals. Write everything down here and you'll be extra-organized plus remember where you're at with the meal prep process.

#3: Choose your meals

Now comes the fun part- you get to choose what you want to eat! Check out the recipes in this book and decide which ones you fancy and will work best for your overall meal plan.

Don't forget that you potentially have three meals per day that you could be planning for, plus a couple of snacks too, so think carefully. Of course, you could start as most people do and just meal prep your lunches. Then as you grow in experience, you can start prepping the rest too.

Depending on whether you're a single person, or you have a whole family to feed, you might want to repeat the meals for several days or mix it up a bit, using different accompaniments, salads, grains, proteins and so on. Don't forget that you can often use dinner recipes at lunchtime, or even breakfast time too. Hell- you can eat cake for breakfast if it says so on your meal prep plan, but that probably wouldn't be the best move for your health!

It's always a good idea to keep it as simple as possible. Many meal preppers like to stick with one staple food when they get started. Things like chicken dishes work really well because they can be prepared many different ways without feeling like you're eating the same food again and again.

Also, try to keep your meals balanced by always following this formula:

Healthy protein + **healthy grain** (*or grain alternative*) + **vegetables or fruit** + **healthy fat**.

This will help ensure you get the nutrients your body needs and enjoy your food to the max.

#4: Choose the right storage container

Yes, you *could* throw everything into one of those big plastic lunchboxes and pop it into the fridge or freezer. But if you're prepping a whole meal with different parts, for example, spaghetti bolognaise with salad and avocado, you'll have a nightmare when it comes to reheating and you'll just end up with a big blog on your plate.

It's much better if you can find some good containers that match the following criteria:

- **Divided into sections**. Bento boxes work well for this.
- **Airtight**. You don't want your food going stale or rotten before you've even eaten it.
- **BPA-free.** If you haven't heard, BPA is super-bad for your body and can leech all kinds of hormone-disrupting chemicals into the food you eat. Just say no, guys! (FYI, plastic that contains BPA has a triangle on it which is printed with the number 7.)
- **Microwavable.** This isn't entirely essential, but it certainly helps when you want to just heat up your food fast with less clean-up afterwards.

- **Clear and easy to label.** Nothing worse than digging out a meal from your fridge or freezer, only to realize you have no clue what's inside. It might not seem like much of a problem when you get started, but as you become a meal prep pro, you'll see what I mean!
- **The same size & easy to stack**. This isn't essential either, but it does mean they'll be easy to stack, easy to use the same portions in each and they'll save valuable storage space.

#5: Write your grocery list and go shopping

Once you've decided what you'll be eating, it's time to make your grocery list. Grab a pen and a piece of paper and write down everything you'll need from the grocery store, including the quantities.

Then head to the store, grocery list in hand, and grab what you need. Don't get distracted by anything else there- just get in and get done.

#6: Get prepping!

Now you just need to get prepping.

Depending on what you're eating, this could involve a whole lot of chopping, peeling, slicing, cooking, sautéing and baking, before dividing it into the right storage containers and storing in the fridge or freezer.

Having said that, you don't have to cook absolutely everything beforehand if you don't want to. Many meal preppers are fan of the 'bag it' approach- they organize their ingredients beforehand and store the correct quantities in zip lock bags. Then when it's time to cook, they can simply empty the ingredients into their Instant Pot and get cooking.

In this book, I've given you full instructions for cooking right away, but that doesn't mean you have to do exactly this. It's your meal prep, after all. You can always bag your ingredients in this way if that's what works for you. If you choose this approach, Instant Pots are great as you can literally throw the ingredients in, cover and leave to cook whilst you take a shower, or whatever else you'd prefer to be doing.

#7: Keep practicing

The longer you spend doing meal prep, the more you'll learn about what works for you and what definitely doesn't. You'll be able to tweak how you do your meal prep to make it more effective and do exactly what it's setting out to achieve- saving you time.

But that doesn't mean you have to accept eating old floppy cucumber slices or apples slices that look brown and suspicious. Prepare the same day if needed, or even cook from fresh if you have the time. It's not a competition!

If this all sounds like a lot to think about, don't worry. With practice, it will all become super-easy.

Chapter 4: What You Need to Know about Your Instant Pot

An Instant Pot is a time-saving kitchen miracle that will help you slash the time you spend in the kitchen and spend more time doing what really matters in life- living your life to the full! Sound familiar? Yep, that's what meal prep does too. Put them together and you have a match made in heaven. But more on that later...

Many people describe Instant Pots as being electric pressure cookers, but I like to think of them as multi-functional cookers that sit on your counter top and help you out in the kitchen.

When it comes to meal prep, it's going to be your secret weapon, the one that takes charge of the tough, time-consuming stuff so you can multitask, creating more dishes in less time and getting more organized than you ever thought possible!

Besides, it's much more than just an electric pressure cooker- you also have a sauté pan, a slow cooker, a rice cooker, a steamer, a yoghurt maker, a warming pot and even an oven that will help you create mouth-watering cakes, cookies and pancakes.

And most importantly of all, your Instant Pot won't just slash the time you take to do all these things- it also maximizes the flavors whilst minimizing the cost. Think melt-off-the-bone meat, tender fish dishes, your favorite veggies and grains cooked to perfection, and much more.

I love mine sooo much that I've gathered together some of the best benefits of using one. Check it out below:

The benefits...

#1: They're slash the time you spend in the kitchen

Yes, I know I've already said this, but it's so important. Because most of us are just too busy to spend hours checking a pork roast in the oven, or stirring dishes that take hours to cook properly, but we still want to enjoy all the flavors we love. Your Instant Pot will let you still enjoy these foods but cut cooking time down to around 70%! Awesome, huh?

#2: You can eat healthy food for less

When you cook for yourself at home instead of buying pre-prepared foods or eating out, you'll be able to stick to your healthy-eating goals with ease. Instead of shopping and eating for convenience and so compromising on health, you can choose exactly what you include with your dishes, you can tweak them to whatever diet or lifestyle you're following and pack as much nutrition into your food as your heart desires! Awesome!

#3: You'll stick to your budget

You already know that meal prep will probably save you a ton of money, but did you know that cooking with an Instant Pot will also help. You can create big batches of food, so you can cut back how much you're spending on groceries. And you'll be organized so you know that you have a delicious meal waiting for you, and you *won't* be tempted to stop at the store on the way home, and load up with unhealthy junk like chips, donuts, cookies and soda.

#4: You'll get more nutrients

Because Instant Pot cooking traps all the moisture inside the cooking chamber, you'll also retain many of the vitamins, minerals and antioxidants that are often lost with traditional cooking techniques. This means healthier you and easier life. Double win!

#5: You can save space!

As I've already mentioned, your Instant Pot will do the job of many other cooking appliances, so you can cut down on the mess in your kitchen and feel calm, tidy and more organized. This means it's especially ideal for smaller homes and apartments.

#6: They're pretty safe

If you've ever used a pressure cooker, you'll know that they can feel slightly scary with all that pressure building up inside. But you don't have to worry with the Instant Pot as the expert design means they have many safety-regulating features to check what's going on. But remember, they can still be hot! Be carefully when opening the lid.

The buttons...

'Whaaat? What are all those buttons for?'

That was my first reaction when I opened up the box my Instant Pot had just been delivered in and peered down at what was inside. But once you understand what they're all for, it's actually super simple.

You basically have two different methods of using your Instant Pot:

1. You use the fancy presets that will help you cook your food with the press of just one button.
2. You use the manual pressure buttons are adjust the cooking time to accurately cook your meal to your requirements.

Whichever of these you end up using is really up to you, but I'd advise to sick with manual controls if you can. After all, not all meats cook at the exact same speed or need to same level of pressure.

For that reason, all the recipes you'll find here are written using the **'low/high pressure'** + **'manual'** + **'cooking time'** method.

If you're not so keen on using this approach, take a look at the quick guide below:

Instant Pot Button Guide

Preset Buttons

- Soup - Cooks for 30 minutes on high pressure
- Meat/stew - Cooks for 35 minutes on high pressure
- Bean/chili - Cooks for 30 minutes on high pressure
- Poultry - Cooks for 15 minutes on high pressure
- Rice - Cooks rice automatically
- Multigrain - Cooks for 40 minutes on high pressure
- Porridge - Cooks for 20 minutes on high pressure
- Steam - Cooks for 10 minutes on high pressure
- Cake - Cooks your favorite cakes (please check manufacturer's guide for times and settings)
- Yoghurt - Helps you create delicious yoghurt
- Egg - Cooks your eggs hard or soft boiled
- Sterilize - Cleans your utensils and jars

The basic buttons

- Sauté - Use this to sauté onions, garlic and vegetables, brown meat, or simmer on a lower heat.
- Keep warm/cancel - Press this to stop cooking or to keep your food warm.
- Manual/pressure cook - This is the setting I refer to throughout the recipe section.
- Slow cooker - This gives a default 4-hour cooking time.
- Pressure - This button allows you to switch between high and low pressure

- Timer - You can delay the start of cooking by using this setting.

Disclaimer: Not all brands of Instant Pot have these settings so don't be worried if you can't find the ones I've mentioned here.

So now we come to the end of Part I. The introductions have been done. I've explained how to meal prep, the steps you need to take to get started, how your Instant Pot can help, and I've also given you a lightning guide to your Instant Pot.

There's just one thing left to do- explore the delicious recipes I've put together for you and start cooking. Join me in the next section and prepare for your mouth to water!

Part II: Meal Prep Instant Pot Recipes

Breakfast

Easy Peel Instant Pot Hard Boiled Eggs

These easy hard- boiled eggs are every meal-prepper's dream come true. They're fast and easy to make, they stay fresh in the fridge for a decent amount of time and they're perfect for a breakfast, lunchtime sandwich, or even a protein-filled snack.

Serves: 6-12
Cooks: 20 mins

Ingredients:
- 1 cup (235ml) water
- 12 free-range eggs
- Ice + water

Method:
1. Place the water into the bottom of your Instant Pot. Drop in the steamer rack.
2. Place eggs onto the rack (in one layer).
3. Cover and cook on manual high for five minutes for hard eggs, or three minutes for soft-boiled eggs.
4. Do a quick pressure release then remove the eggs.
5. Drop into a bowl of iced water and leave for 5-10 minutes.
6. Peel and store in the fridge until you want to eat them! They store for around a week.

Oatmeal in a Jar

Love the convenience of overnight oats but want something creamier and more filling for your brekkie? Check out these awesome Instant Pot oats. They're packed with flavor, bursting with superfoods and will set you up for breakfast all week long.

Serves: 5
Cooks: 10

Ingredients:
- 1 ¼ cup (115g) rolled oats
- 3 cups (705ml) milk
- 1/3 cup (80ml) cream
- 1 apple, chopped (or to taste)
- 1 large carrot, shredded
- 1/3 cup (50g) raisins or goji berries
- ½ cup (60g) chopped walnuts
- ¼ cup (80g) flaxseed or chia seed
- ½ Tbsp. cinnamon
- Pinch of sea salt

To serve...
- 4 Tbsp. coconut sugar or maple syrup (opt.)
- Fresh Blueberries

Method:
1. Place the milk into your Instant Pot, followed by the cream and stir well to combine.
2. Add the remaining ingredients then cover.
3. Cook on manual high for 7 minutes.
4. Do a quick pressure release and allow to cool.
5. Divide between your storage containers and pop into the fridge until you're ready to serve.
6. On eating day, either enjoy cold with the blueberries and sugar, or add a touch of water and reheat in a pan or in the microwave.

Breakfast Quinoa

Get more bang for your buck with protein-rich quinoa for your breakfast. The basic version is wonderfully simple and easy to throw together, but you can pimp it up however you like for awesome breakfasts throughout the week. Yum!

Serves: 6
Cooks: 15 mins

Ingredients:
- 1 ½ cups (280g) uncooked quinoa, well rinsed
- 2 ¼ cups (530ml) water
- 2 Tbsp. maple syrup
- ½ tsp. vanilla
- ¼ tsp. ground cinnamon
- Pinch of salt

To serve...
- Milk
- Fresh berries
- Sliced almonds

Method:
1. Place all the ingredients (except the toppings) into your Instant Pot.
2. Cover and cook on manual high for one minute.
3. Do a natural pressure release for 10 minutes then a quick pressure release.
4. Allow to cool slightly before dividing between your storage containers and storing in the fridge until you're ready to use.
5. On serving day, eat cold or gently warm in the microwave, top with whatever you like and enjoy!

Fajita Breakfast Casserole

If you'd prefer to steer clear of carbs and would prefer something tasty and satisfying to start your day, put this Fajita breakfast casserole on the list. As the name would suggest, it's Mexican-inspired and tastes great with lashings of chili sauce. Feel free to double your batch if your Instant Pot has enough space.

Serves: 2
Cooks: 12 mins

Ingredients:

- ½ cup (75g) onion
- 1 ½ cup (150g) sliced bell peppers
- 1 Tbsp. olive oil
- 4 free range eggs
- Salt and pepper, to taste
- 1 cup (235ml) water

To serve...

- Cilantro
- Tabasco sauce

Method:

1. Open your Instant Pot, turn onto sauté and add the oil.
2. Add the onions, garlic and peppers and cook for around 5 minutes.
3. Remove from the Instant Pot and turn off the heat.
4. Grab a round pan that will fit inside your Instant Pot, grease and transfer the onion mixture to the pan,
5. Crack the eggs and pour on top of the peppers. Keep the egg whole if you can.
6. Season well then cover.
7. Place the trivet into the Instant Pot and add the water.
8. Lower the pan inside and close the lid.
9. Cook on manual high for two minutes then do a quick pressure release.
10. Remove and allow to cool before dividing between your storage containers.
11. On serving day, enjoy with a slice or two of toast, sliced avocados, cilantro and whatever other topping your heart desires.

Crustless Crab Quiche

There's something about crab quiche that makes me go weak at the knees, so it's a real treat to start my day with a hearty portion of this rich and creamy creation. You can make this a great dairy-free dish by subbing the half and half with coconut cream...Wow!

Serves: 4
Cooks: 50 mins

Ingredients:
- 4 free range eggs
- 1 cup (20ml) half and half
- ½ tsp. salt
- 1 tsp. pepper
- 1 tsp. sweet smoked paprika
- 1 tsp. Herbes de Provence
- 1 cup (125g) shredded Parmesan or Swiss cheese
- 1 cup (150g) chopped green onions green and white parts
- 8 oz. (225g) crab meat (real or imitation)
- 2 cups (470ml) water

Method:
1. Grab a bowl and whisk together all the ingredients except the water, onions and crab meat.
2. Stir in the crab and onions.
3. Find a springform pan that will fit inside your Instant Pot and line with foil.
4. Pour the quiche mixture inside the pan.
5. Open your Instant Pot, drop in the trivet and add the water.
6. Drop the pan inside and cover.
7. Cook on manual high for 40 minutes.
8. Do a natural pressure release for 10 minutes then a quick pressure release.
9. Remove from the Instant Pot and allow to cool before dividing between your storage boxes and storing the fridge.
10. On serving day, enjoy cold or warm gently in the microwave.

Fresh Berry Compote

Give your oatmeal, yoghurt or granola a facelift or simply bring the taste of summer to your taste buds with this delicious stewed fruit. Make a batch, keep it in your fridge and you'll have enough to last you for days! Feel free to substitute the berries for whatever fruit you have on hand- it will still taste awesome.

Serves: 4
Cooks: 5 mins

Ingredients:
- 1 lb. (450g) fresh strawberries washed, trimmed and cut in half
- 1 lb. (450g) fresh blueberries washed
- 4 Tbsp. sugar
- 2 tsp. orange juice

To serve...
- Vanilla bean
- Whole nutmeg
- Ground cinnamon

Method:
1. Place the fruit into your Instant Pot and sprinkle with sugar. Leave to rest for 20-30 minutes.
2. Add the orange juice, cover and cook on high for one minute.
3. Do a natural pressure release for 15 minutes then do a quick pressure release.
4. Allow it to cool and watch how deliciously it thickens!
5. Once cool, divide between storage containers and pop into the fridge until needed. You can also freeze this compote if required.

Jamaican Cornmeal Porridge

Ever tried Jamaican cornmeal porridge? No? Then you're in for a real treat. Spicy, satisfying and oh-so good, this stuff could become your new breakfast go-to.

Serves: 4
Cooks: 25 mins

Ingredients:

- 4 cups (940ml) water
- 1 cup (235ml) milk
- 1 cup fine yellow cornmeal
- 2 sticks cinnamon
- 3 pimento berries
- 1 tsp. vanilla extract
- ½ tsp. nutmeg, ground

To serve...

- ½ cup (120ml) sweetened condensed milk

Method:

1. Add three cups of the water and the milk to your Instant Pot.
2. Grab a separate bowl and add the cornmeal and remaining water. Whisk well to combine.
3. Pour this into the milk mixture and whisk again.
4. Add the remaining ingredients, cover and cook on manual high for 6 minutes.
5. Do a natural pressure release.
6. Open and allow to cool before dividing between storage pots and popping into the fridge.
7. On serving day, warm gently in a pan or the microwave, then serve and enjoy. It takes amazing with the sweetened condensed milk, or whatever else you fancy!

Breakfast Cobbler

For a breakfast with a real difference, try out this indulgent breakfast cobbler. Again, you can substitute whatever fruit is in season, switch the coconut oil for butter and give your own special touch to the dish to make it epic!

Serves: 4
Cooks: 15 mins

Ingredients:

- 2 pears, diced
- 2 apples, diced
- 2 plums, diced
- 4 Tbsp. (60 ml) local honey
- 6 Tbsp. (90 ml) coconut oil
- 1 tsp. ground cinnamon
- ½ cup (38 g) unsweetened shredded coconut
- ½ cup (60 g) pecan pieces
- 4 Tbsp. (40 g) sunflower seeds

To serve...

- Whipped cream

Method:

1. Place the fruit, honey, coconut oil and cinnamon into your Instant Pot.
2. Cover with the lid and cook on manual high for 10 minutes.
3. Do a quick pressure release and carefully open.
4. Transfer the fruit to a serving bowl to cool but leave the liquid in the pan.
5. Add the coconut, pecans and sunflower seeds into the liquid, press the sauté button and cook for 5 minutes, stirring often.
6. When the fruit and seed mixture are cool, transfer to a storage container until ready to use.
7. On serving day, gently warm the fruit mixture in the microwave and cover with the seed mixture, then top with the cream. Yum!

Cinnamon Monkey Bread

Monkey bread is one of those breakfasts you think is too indulgent to enjoy for breakfast, but you end up eating day after day! I think we all deserve to enjoy it whenever we like. But be warned, when you try this easy Instant Pot version, you might forget to store it for your meal prep and eat it all there and then whilst it's warm…Well, that's what 'desserts' are for, right?

Serves: 2
Cooks: 21 mins

Ingredients:
- 1 can Southern Buttermilk Grands biscuits (or alternative of your choice)
- ½ cup (170g) white sugar
- 1 ½ tsp. cinnamon
- ½ stick butter
- ½ cup light brown sugar
- 1 piece of foil
- 1 cup (235ml) water

Method:
1. Grab a large bowl and add the white sugar and cinnamon. Stir well.
2. Cut eight biscuits into quarters and add to the sugar mix. Stir well to coat.
3. Grab two mini loaf pans (that will fit into your Instant Pot) and place half of the biscuit mixture in each.
4. Next pop the butter and sugar into a small bowl and place into the microwave until melted. This should take around 30 seconds. Stir well and pour over the biscuits.
5. Place the trivet into the bottom of your Instant Pot, add the water and place the loaf pans on top. Cover with a piece of foil.
6. Cover and cook on manual high for 21 minutes.
7. Do a natural pressure release for 5 minutes then a quick pressure release.
8. Open the lid, remove the pans and leave to cool.
9. Once cooled, transfer into storage containers or bags and pop straight into the freezer.
10. On serving day, remove from the freezer several hours before to defrost or pop into the microwave for a few seconds.

Breakfast Egg Muffins with Parmesan, Spinach, and Tomatoes

These cute egg muffins are a cut above your average egg breakfast. Bursting with fresh Italian flavors and lifted with a generous amount of parmesan, they're also extremely addictive. They also make a great quick sandwich when sliced and popped into your favorite bread with whatever toppings you love.

Serves: 6
Cooks: 30 mins

Ingredients:
- Non-stick cooking spray
- 8 free-range eggs
- ¼ cup (60 ml milk)
- ¼ tsp. salt
- 1/8 tsp. fresh ground black pepper
- 1 cup (30 g) fresh baby spinach, chopped
- ½ cup (90 g) diced seeded tomato
- 2 scallions white and green parts, sliced
- 1/3 cup (30g) shredded Parmesan cheese
- 1 cup (235ml) water

Method:
1. Find six heat-proof mugs and spray with the cooking spray.
2. Then grab a large bowl and add the eggs, milk, salt and pepper. Whisk until blended.
3. Place the spinach, tomato and scallions into the mugs, dividing between the six mugs.
4. Pour the egg mixture into the cups over the veggies and top with the Parmesan.
5. Place the water into the Instant Pot, drop the trivet into the bottom and place the mugs inside.
6. Cover and cook on manual high for six minutes.
7. Do a natural pressure release for five minutes, then a quick pressure release.
8. Remove the lid and carefully remove the cups.
9. Allow to cool completely then store in the fridge until ready to serve.
10. On serving day, warm gently in the microwave or enjoy cold!

Spiced Apple Steel Cut Oats

The scent of spiced apples always takes me back to my childhood when I'd find my mother stirring a massive pot on the stove, singing at the top of her voice! So, I decided to combine my love of oatmeal with my love for my mother to create this yummy breakfast treat.

Serves: 4
Cooks: 20 mins

Ingredients:

- 1 1/3 cup (170g) steel cut oats
- 4 cups (940ml) water
- 1 tsp. cinnamon
- ¼ tsp. ground nutmeg
- ¼ tsp. ground ginger
- ¼ tsp. all-spice
- 2 apples, chopped

To serve...

- Maple syrup
- Butter
- Chopped nuts

Method:

1. Place the ingredients into your Instant Pot, give it a stir then cover.
2. Cook for 3 minutes on manual high pressure.
3. Do a natural pressure release for ten minutes then do a quick pressure release.
4. Allow to cool then divide between storage containers and pop into the fridge until you're ready to enjoy them.
5. On serving day, gently warm in the microwave, top with whatever toppings take your fancy, then serve and enjoy!

Cheesy Egg Bake

Hash browns, eggs, cheese, bacon...you can't really go wrong, can you? Throw in whatever veggies you have left over from last night's dinner and you'll have all the food groups in one bite. Mmmm....

Serves: 4
Cooks: 25 mins

Ingredients:
- 6 slices bacon, chopped
- 2 cups (260g) frozen hash browns
- 6 free-range eggs
- ¼ cup (60ml) milk
- ½ cup (60g) shredded cheddar cheese
- 1 tsp. salt
- ½ tsp. pepper
- A selection of veggies: onion, red pepper, spinach, mushrooms, green onions (to taste)
- 1 cup (235ml) water

Method:
1. Turn your Instant Pot onto sauté and cook the bacon until crispy.
2. Add your chosen veggies and cook for five minutes until tender.
3. Add the hash browns and stir well until starting to thaw.
4. Grease a heatproof bowl that will fit into your Instant Pot and add the cooked bacon and veggie mixture.
5. Grab a bowl, whisk together the eggs, milk, shredded cheese and salt and pepper, then pour over the veggies.
6. Pop the water into your Instant Pot, add the water and drop in the trivet.
7. Place the bowl inside your Instant Pot, cover and cook on manual high for 20 minutes.
8. Do a quick pressure release then carefully open.
9. Allow to cool completely then divide between your storage containers.
10. On serving day, warm gently in the microwave then serve and enjoy!

Soups and Stews

Golden Lentil and Spinach Soup

What do you get when you combine tender, protein-rich lentils with a bunch of flavorful veggies, some carefully-chosen spices and a whole lot of love?? A delicious, satisfying soup that will give you enough lunches to last nearly a week, or even make a great simple supper when you don't feel like cooking.

Serves: 4
Cooks: 35 mins

Ingredients:
- 2 tsp. olive oil
- ½ medium yellow onion, diced
- 2 medium carrots, peeled and diced
- 1 medium stalk celery, diced
- 4 medium cloves garlic, minced
- 2 tsp. ground cumin
- 1 tsp. ground turmeric
- 1 tsp. dried thyme
- 1 tsp. salt + more to taste
- ¼ tsp. freshly ground black pepper+ more to taste
- 1 cup (200g) dry brown lentils, rinsed well in cold water
- 4 cups (940ml) low-sodium vegetable broth
- 8 oz. (225g) baby spinach

Method:
1. Turn your Instant Pot onto sauté and add the oil.
2. Add the onions, carrots and celery and cook for around 5 minutes until beginning to soften. Stir often.
3. Next throw in the garlic, cumin, turmeric, thyme, salt, and pepper, and cook for another minute or so.
4. Add the lentils and the broth and stir, then cover and cook on manual high for 12 minutes.
5. Do a quick release, then open the lid and add the spinach, plus any extra seasoning you think it needs.

6. Allow to cool completely before dividing between storage containers. This will keep for around three days in the fridge, or you can pop it in your freezer and store for up to a month.

7. On serving day, remove from the freezer well ahead of time (if storing it there), then gently warm in a pan or in the microwave.

Beef and Butternut Squash Stew

Ok, I won't lie about this one- it really is something very special. Beef and butternut squash are a match made in heaven, and when lifted with sweet paprika, thyme and rosemary and a handful of tasty veggies, you'll just keep coming back for more. This one makes a lot, so it's perfect for families, or for throwing into the freezer for a rainy day.

Serves: 10
Cooks: 45 mins

Ingredients:
- 1 large onion
- 2 cloves garlic
- 2 celery stalks
- 2 carrots
- 2 Tbsp. tomato paste
- 1 Tbsp. breadcrumbs
- 2 lb. (900g) beef stew
- 4 Tbsp. arrowroot starch
- 6 cups (1.2kg) peeled and chopped butternut squash
- ½ cup (120ml) Marsala wine
- 2 ½ cups (590ml) beef broth
- 3 tablespoons extra virgin olive oil
- 2 bay leaves
- 1 tsp. sweet Hungarian paprika
- 1 tsp. thyme
- 1 tsp. rosemary

Method:
1. Turn your Instant Pot onto sauté and add the oil.
2. Add the onions, garlic, celery and carrots. Cook for around 5 minutes until beginning to soften. Stir often.
3. Next add the tomato, tomato paste and seasoning. Stir well.
4. Grab your beef and season with salt, pepper and arrowroot. Throw into the Instant Pot with the butternut squash.
5. Throw in the remaining ingredients, stir well and cover.
6. Cook on manual high for 30 minutes.
7. Do a quick pressure release and carefully open up.

8. Allow to cool completely before dividing between storage containers. You can pop it into the fridge for up to three days, or store in your freezer for around a month.
9. On serving day, remove from the freezer well ahead of time (if storing it there), then gently warm in a pan or in the microwave.

Simple Tortilla Soup

I love the way that this tortilla soup is so simple, but it's soooo delicious too. The spicy chicken and tomato base is to die for, and you can jazz it up with whatever toppings you like. I've included my personal faves here to get you inspired.

Serves: 4
Cooks: 45 mins

Ingredients:

- 8 cups (1.9 liters) bone broth
- 1 Tbsp. oil
- 1 pasilla chili (can substitute with chili of your choice if you prefer)
- 1 onion
- 3 garlic cloves
- 1 x 28 oz. (793g) can diced tomatoes
- 1 spring cilantro, plus more for garnish
- 1 tsp. cumin
- 1 lb. (450g) chicken (boneless breasts or thighs)
- Salt & pepper, to taste

To serve...

- Avocado
- Cheddar cheese
- Corn tortillas (cut into strips and toasted)
- Lime wedges

Method:

1. Turn your Instant Pot onto sauté and add the oil.
2. Add the onions and garlic and cook for around 5 minutes until beginning to soften. Stir often.
3. Throw in the chili and sauté for a minute or so.
4. Next add the chicken and brown on each side for around 5 minutes.
5. Add the tomatoes, cilantro, cumin, broth and salt and pepper. Stir well.
6. Cover and cook on manual high for 20 minutes.
7. Do a quick pressure release then open up.
8. Remove the chicken from the pot and gently shred with two forks before returning to the pot.

9. Allow to cool completely before dividing between storage containers. You can pop it into the fridge for up to three days, or store in your freezer for around a month.
10. On serving day, remove from the freezer well ahead of time (if storing it there), then gently warm in a pan or in the microwave. Top with extras like avocados, cheese, toasted tortillas and enjoy!

Split Pea Soup

This split pea soup recipe comes courtesy of my late grandmother who was a great believer of saving time in the kitchen, but also wanted to keep everyone healthy and strong. It has a gentle sweetness, plenty of taste, tons of protein and all the garlicky goodness you could ever want. Enjoy!

Serves: 6
Cooks: 30 mins

Ingredients:

- 40 fl.oz. (1.2 liters) vegetable stock
- 2 cups (450g) split peas dry, uncooked
- ½ onion, diced
- 2 carrots, sliced
- 2 stalks celery, sliced
- 2 Tbsp. olive oil
- 1 ½ tsp. salt (or to taste)
- 1 tsp. garlic powder
- 1 cup (150g) ham, diced

Method:

1. Turn your Instant Pot onto sauté and add the oil.
2. Add the onions and ham. Cook for around 5 minutes until beginning to soften. Stir often.
3. Throw in the remaining ingredients, season, stir and cover with the lid.
4. Cook on manual high pressure for 17 minutes, then do a quick pressure release.
5. Allow to cool completely before dividing between storage containers. You can pop it into the fridge for up to three days, or store in your freezer for around a month.
6. On serving day, remove from the freezer well ahead of time (if storing it there), then gently warm in a pan or in the microwave.

Vegan Curried Butternut Squash Soup

You know those days when you're craving creamy, warming and tasty above all
Then turn to this curried butternut squash soup. The creaminess comes from coconut
milk here, but you can always switch to an alternative or dairy cream if you're not a
vegan or you're not a big fan of coconut.

Serves: 4
Cooks: 50 mins

Ingredients:
- 1 tsp. extra-virgin olive oil
- 1 large onion
- 2 cloves garlic
- 1 Tbsp. curry powder
- 3 lb. (1.4 kg) butternut squash, chopped and peeled
- 1 ½ tsp. fine sea salt
- 3 cups (705ml) water
- ½ cup (120ml) coconut milk

To serve...
- Hulled pumpkin seeds
- Dried cranberries

Method:
1. Turn your Instant Pot onto sauté and add the oil.
2. Add the onions and cook for around 5 minutes until beginning to soften. Stir often.
3. Throw in the garlic and curry powder, then cook for another minute or so.
4. Turn off the Instant Pot and add the squash, salt and water. Stir well.
5. Cover and cook on manual high for 30 minutes.
6. Do a natural pressure release for 10 minutes then do a quick pressure release.
7. Use an immersion blender to blend the soup until as smooth as you love it, then add the coconut milk.
8. Allow to cool completely before dividing between storage containers. You can pop it into the fridge for up to a week, or store in your freezer for around a month.
9. On serving day, remove from the freezer well ahead of time (if storing it there), then gently warm in a pan or in the microwave. Top with the pumpkin seeds and cranberries, or whatever else you fancy, then enjoy!

Spicy Instant Pot Beef & Lentil Stew

You could claim that the mouth-watering flavor of this one comes from the thyme and oregano. You could claim it comes from the mushroom-carrot-beef combo. But I know the truth. It comes from one place alone- how much love you put into making it. It might sound crazy, but you know it's true.

Serves: 4-6
Cooks: 35 mins

Ingredients:
- 2 lb. (900g) beef stew meat, cut into bit size pieces
- 1 tsp. pepper
- 2 x 10 oz. (285g) cans Rotel tomatoes
- 2 Tbsp. Beef Bouillon Powder
- 1 onion, diced
- 4 garlic cloves, diced
- 1 tsp. dried thyme
- 1 tsp. dried oregano
- 1 cup (200g) dried green lentils
- 2 cups (260g) chopped carrots
- 2 cups (150g) halved mushrooms
- 4 cups (940ml) water
- Flour slurry – 4 Tbsp. flour plus 4 Tbsp. water

Method:
1. Open your Instant Pot and add the beef, pepper, diced tomatoes, bouillon powder, thyme, oregano, garlic and onion.
2. Add the water then stir well. Cover and cook on manual high pressure for 30 minutes.
3. Do a quick pressure release then open up.
4. Add the lentils, carrots and mushrooms and stir well to combine.
5. Cover and cook on manual high pressure for five minutes.
6. Do a natural pressure release for 10 minutes, then a quick pressure release.
7. Open up the lid and add the flour slurry, then stir well.
8. Allow to cool completely before dividing between storage containers. You can pop it into the fridge for up to a week, or store in your freezer for around a month.
9. On serving day, remove from the freezer well ahead of time (if storing it there), then gently warm in a pan or in the microwave.

Mexican Chicken Stew

If you're a fan of spicy food, you'll want to make sure you add the right ingredients to your grocery list, so you can look forward to a nutritious, satisfying stew any night of the week. And honesty, once you pile on the toppings you'll have much more than an easy meal- you'll have something you can really look forward to.

Serves: 8
Cooks: 30 mins

Ingredients:
- 2 carrots, diced
- 1 medium onion, diced
- 1 green pepper, diced
- 1 Tbsp. olive oil
- 8 chicken thighs
- 1 can (340g) corn
- 1 x 19 oz. (540ml) can black beans
- 1 x 4.3 oz. (120g) can green chilis
- ¾ cup (200g) salsa
- 1 ½ cups (350ml) chicken stock
- 1 tsp. ground cumin
- 1 tsp. chili powder

To serve...
- 2 tsp. lime juice
- ¼ tsp. salt
- 1 cup (125g) shredded cheddar cheese
- 1 avocado, cubed
- ½ cup (125g) Greek yogurt or sour cream
- Tortilla chips

Method:
1. Turn your Instant Pot onto sauté and add the oil.
2. Add the onions, carrots and bell pepper and cook for around 5 minutes until beginning to soften. Stir often.
3. Add the chicken and cook for another five minutes until starting to brown, then turn off your Instant Pot.
4. Add the remaining ingredients (apart from the salt and lime) and stir well.

43

5. Cover and cook on manual high pressure for six minutes.
6. Do a natural pressure release for 10 minutes, then a quick pressure release.
7. Open up and stir through the lime and salt.
8. Allow to cool completely before dividing between storage containers. You can pop it into the fridge for up to a week, or store in your freezer for around a month.
9. On serving day, remove from the freezer well ahead of time (if storing it there), then gently warm in a pan or in the microwave.
10. Serve with a topping of your choice!

Pork Goulash

I was never such a big fan of goulash until I tried this easy Instant Pot version. And since I did I've been hooked! The two types of paprika make it incredibly rich and tasty, the pork keeps your tummy happy and the veggies reassure you that you're eating great food and still getting your five-a-day.

Serves: 8
Cooks: 45 mins

Ingredients:
- 1 lb. (450g) pork loin, chopped into cubes
- 4 Tbsp. canola oil
- 3 medium onions, chopped
- 8 garlic cloves, minced
- 1 Tbsp. hot smoked paprika
- 1 Tbsp. sweet paprika
- 2 cups (470ml) beef stock or chicken stock
- 1 cup (235ml) cold water
- 1 x 14.5 oz. (410g) diced tomatoes
- 2 Tbsp. tomato paste
- 4 bay leaves
- 2 rosemary sticks
- 2 red bell peppers, chopped
- 5 medium carrots, cleaned and chopped
- Salt and pepper, to taste

Method:
1. Turn your Instant Pot onto sauté and add the oil.
2. Add the meat and cook for around 5 minutes until it starts to brown, stirring often.
3. Next add the onions and garlic and cook for a further few minutes.
4. Throw in the carrot, peppers, bay leaves, beef stock, rosemary, water and seasoning.
5. Cover and cook on manual high pressure for 30 minutes.
6. Do a natural pressure release for 10 minutes, then a quick pressure release.
7. Open up and allow to cool completely before dividing between storage containers. You can pop it into the fridge for up to a week, or store in your freezer for around a month.
8. On serving day, remove from the freezer well ahead of time (if storing it there), then gently warm in a pan or in the microwave.
9. Serve with a topping of your choice!

Chicken Chile Verde Soup

This soup is a wonderful cross between a chili and a chicken soup. Bursting with white beans, chilis and yummy Salsa Verde, you'll want to keep piling it onto your plate. So, make sure you give yourself generous portions for the week! Make sure you grab a big hunk of crusty bread to go with it...

Serves: 8
Cooks: 45 mins

Ingredients:
- 3 chicken breasts
- 1 Tbsp. oil
- 1 can black beans
- 19 oz. (540g) cannellini beans, drained and rinsed
- 1 x 4.3 oz. (127g) can green chilis
- 1 x 11.5 oz. (340g) can corn kernels, drained
- 1 onion, diced
- 3 cloves garlic minced
- 2 cup (520ml) Salsa Verde
- 2 tsp. ground cumin
- 1 tsp. ground coriander
- 1 tsp. salt
- 4 cups (940ml) chicken stock
- 3 Tbsp. cornmeal
- Juice of 1 lime

To serve...
- Yogurt
- Cilantro
- Tortilla chips
- Shredded cheese

Method:
1. Turn your Instant Pot onto sauté and add the oil.
2. Add the onions and garlic and cook for around 5 minutes until they start to soften, stirring often.
3. Add the spices and cook for another minute or so until getting fragrant.

4. Throw in the remaining ingredients, except the cornmeal and lime juice, and stir well.
5. Cover and cook on manual high pressure for 10 minutes.
6. Do a quick pressure release, and carefully remove the chicken. Shred with two forks before returning to the pot.
7. Add the cornmeal and lime, then stir through.
8. Allow to cool completely before dividing between storage containers. You can pop it into the fridge for up to a week, or store in your freezer for around a month.
9. On serving day, remove from the freezer well ahead of time (if storing it there), then gently warm in a pan or in the microwave.
10. Serve with your favorite toppings and enjoy!

Ethiopian Chicken Stew with Lentils and Sweet Potato

Just because I'm meal prepping, that doesn't mean I'm willing to compromise on either taste or variety. That's why I love exploring global flavors, like this chicken stew from Ethiopia. If you can get hold of Berbere spice mix, it's worth the effort. Otherwise just sub with cayenne or your favorite chili. Be warned- this stuff is hot!

Serves: 8
Cooks: 45 mins

Ingredients:
- 2 Tbsp. butter
- 1 onion finely diced
- 2 Tbsp. Berbere spice mix (can substitute with cayenne pepper)
- ½ tsp. ground cardamom
- 2 tsp. paprika
- 1 Tbsp. minced ginger
- 3 cloves garlic minced
- 2 carrots peeled and sliced
- 2 ribs celery sliced
- 2 cups (400g) sweet potatoes peeled and cubed
- 2 chicken breasts
- 1 cup (200g) green split lentils dried
- 1 x 19 oz. (540ml) diced tomatoes (including juices)
- 1 cup chicken stock after cooking
- Juice from ½ a lemon
- 1 tsp. brown sugar
- Salt, to taste

Method:
1. Turn your Instant Pot onto sauté and add the butter.
2. Add the onions and garlic and cook for around 5 minutes until they start to soften, stirring often.
3. Throw in the spices and cook for another minute or so.
4. Finally, add the remaining ingredients, stir well then cover.
5. Cook on manual high pressure for 20 minutes.
6. Do a natural pressure release for ten minutes, then a quick pressure release.

7. Allow to cool completely before dividing between storage containers. You can pop it into the fridge for up to a week, or store in your freezer for around a month.
8. On serving day, remove from the freezer well ahead of time (if storing it there), then gently warm in a pan or in the microwave.
9. Serve with your favorite toppings and enjoy!

Smoky Vegan Split Pea Soup with Sweet Potatoes and Navy Beans

I love this split pea soup because it's wonderfully simple, takes just a handful of ingredients and doesn't try to claim to be anything other than what it is- delicious vegan soup. Feel free to throw in some ham if you're not vegan or pimp your soup with anything else you fancy.

Serves: 4-6
Cooks: 40 mins

Ingredients:
- 5 cups (1.2 liters) water
- 1 medium sweet potato, diced
- 1 cup (225g) split peas
- ½ cup (130g) dried navy beans or other white bean of your choice
- 3 bay leaves
- ½ tsp. liquid smoke
- ¼ to ½ cup nutritional yeast, to taste
- Salt and pepper, to taste

Method:
1. Open up your Instant Pot and add all the ingredients except the nutritional yeast, salt and pepper.
2. Stir well, cover and cook on manual high pressure for 20 minutes.
3. Do a natural pressure release then open and stir through the seasoning and the nutritional yeast.
4. Allow to cool completely before dividing between storage containers. You can pop it into the fridge for up to a week, or store in your freezer for around a month.
5. On serving day, remove from the freezer well ahead of time (if storing it there), then gently warm in a pan or in the microwave.
6. Serve with your favorite toppings and enjoy!

Indo-Chinese Corn Soup

Love Asian food? Love veggies? Want to keep things simple and quick? Then you'll love this corn soup. It's ready fast, packed with nutrition and can't help but remind you of vacations in sunny places.

Serves: 4
Cooks: 30 mins

Ingredients:
- 5 cups (1.2 liters) vegetable broth
- 2 ½ cups (440g) corn kernels
- 1 cup (75g) shredded carrot
- 1 cup (340g) shredded cabbage
- 1 Tbsp. tamari or soy sauce
- 2 tsp. sesame oil
- 2 tsp. grated ginger
- 2 tsp. minced garlic
- 1 ½ tsp. ground cumin
- Pepper, to taste

Method:
1. Throw all the ingredients into your Instant Pot, stir well and cover.
2. Cook on manual high pressure for ten minutes.
3. Do a natural pressure release then use an immersion blender to blend the soup to taste. I like plenty of chunks in this one!
4. Adjust the seasoning if required then leave to cool completely.
5. Once cool, divide between storage containers. You can pop it into the fridge for up to a week, or store in your freezer for around a month.
6. On serving day, remove from the freezer well ahead of time (if storing it there), then gently warm in a pan or in the microwave.
7. Serve with your favorite toppings and enjoy!

Spicy Tomato Soup

When it's cold outside, perhaps it's snowing, you're at work and all you want to do is get home and get warm, make sure you have this spicy tomato soup to look forward to. It's super-healthy, easy to make and it keeps well in the fridge for ages. It also makes a great lunchtime treat or starter when you have friends over to eat.

Serves: 2-4
Cooks: 15 mins

Ingredients:
- 1 onion, diced
- 2 garlic cloves, minced
- 1 Tbsp. oil
- 1 x 28 oz. (795g) can tomatoes
- 2 cups tomato stock
- 2 sundried tomatoes, chopped
- 2 Tbsp. tomato paste
- 1 tsp. chipotle puree
- 1 date, pitted
- 2 tsp. salt
- 1 tsp. dried basil
- 1 tsp. dried thyme
- 1 tsp. dried oregano
- ¼ tsp. black pepper

To serve...
- Cream

Method:
1. Turn your Instant Pot onto sauté and add the oil.
2. Add the onions and garlic and cook for around 5 minutes until they start to soften, stirring often.
3. Add the remaining ingredients and stir well.
4. Cover and cook on manual high pressure for five minutes.
5. Do a quick pressure release and open the lid.
6. Use an immersion blender and blend until smooth.
7. Allow to cool completely before dividing between storage containers and popping into the fridge or freezer.
8. On serving day, remove from the freezer well ahead of time (if storing it there), then gently warm in a pan or in the microwave.
9. Serve with your favorite toppings and enjoy!

Seafood Gumbo

Speaking of having friends over, if you want to impress the crowds but want to keep cooking effort to a minimum, why not try this excellent seafood gumbo. All you need is a bunch of seafood, some veggies, some seasoning, some tomatoes and your trusty Instant Pot and you're ready for kitchen domination!

Serves: 8
Cooks: 30 mins

Ingredients:
- 24 oz. (680g) sea bass cut into chunks
- 3 Tbsp. oil
- 3 Tbsp. Cajun or Creole seasoning
- 2 yellow onions diced
- 2 bell peppers diced
- 4 celery ribs diced
- 28 oz. (795g) diced tomatoes
- 4 Tbsp. tomato paste
- 3 bay leaves
- 1 ½ cups (355ml) bone broth
- 2 lb. (900g) medium to large raw shrimp deveined
- Sea salt to taste black pepper to taste

Method:
1. Start by seasoning the sea bass with salt and pepper, then any seasonings you've chosen to use.
2. Turn your Instant Pot onto sauté and add the oil.
3. Add the sea bass chunks and cook for around four minutes until cooked. Remove and place on a plate.
4. Next add the onions, pepper, celery and any remaining seasoning to the pan. Cook for two minutes.
5. Add the tomatoes, tomato paste, bay leaves and broth and stir well.
6. Cover and cook on manual high pressure for five minutes.
7. Do a quick pressure release then add the shrimp. Cook on sauté for three or four minutes until the shrimp is cooked through.
8. Turn off and allow to cool completely.

9. Allow to cool completely before dividing between storage containers and popping into the fridge or freezer.
10. On serving day, remove from the freezer well ahead of time (if storing it there), then gently warm in a pan or in the microwave. Serve with your favorite toppings and enjoy!

Appetizers & Side Dishes

Mexican Rice

Rice dishes like this tasty Mexican version are a wonderful secret weapon when you're meal prepping for the week but want to maximize the taste. This makes six generous portions of rice which go well with any lunchbox or main meal. Who am I kidding? I've even been known to enjoy this one as a snack, straight from the fridge. Yum!

Serves: 6
Cooks: 35 mins

Ingredients:
- 2 cups (370g) long-grain white rice
- ½ white onion, chopped
- 8 Tbsp. tomato paste
- 3 cloves garlic, minced)
- 1 small jalapeño (optional)
- 2 tsp. salt
- 2 cups (470ml) water

Method:
1. Turn your Instant Pot onto sauté and add the oil.
2. Add the onions and garlic and cook for around 5 minutes until they start to soften, stirring often.
3. Add the rice, stir well and toast for a further minute.
4. Add the water, tomato paste and whole jalapeño, then stir well and cover.
5. Cook on manual high for three minutes.
6. Do a natural pressure release for 15 minutes then do a quick pressure release.
7. Open the lid and allow to cool completely before diving between storage containers.
8. Pop into the fridge until ready to eat. (You can also freeze this rice, but it's not always easy to reheat it well).

Sweet Potatoes

es are so simple in the Instant Pot and they also store well in the fridge for ys' worth of lunches. Don't worry if they discolor slightly whilst stored- this is perfectly normal.

Serves: 4
Cooks: 30 mins

Ingredients:
- 4 sweet potatoes
- 1 ½ cup (355ml) water

Method:
1. Wash your potatoes and trim as necessary.
2. Pour the water into your Instant Pot, drop in the trivet and add the potatoes.
3. Cover and cook on manual high for 18 minutes.
4. Do a natural pressure release.
5. Open up and remove the potatoes.
6. Allow to cool completely before popping into storage containers and placing into the fridge.
7. Use within a week.
8. To reheat, pop into the microwave or preheated oven for a few minutes.

Lime Cilantro Rice

Here's another rice dish for you, but not as plain as you might think. The secret lies in the addition of the lime juice and the cilantro. You'll see!

Serves: 2-3
Cooks: 20 mins

Ingredients:

- 1 cup (185g) white rice
- 1 ½ cups (355ml) water

To serve...

- Juice and zest of one lime
- 4 Tbsp. chopped cilantro
- Salt, to taste

Method:

1. Place the rice and water into your Instant Pot.
2. Cover and cook on manual low pressure for 12 minutes.
3. Do a quick pressure release and remove the lid.
4. Fluff with a fork and stir through the remaining ingredients.
5. Allow to cool completely before dividing between storage containers and popping into the fridge or freezer.
6. On serving day, gently warm in a preheated or in the microwave. You can also serve if cold if you like.

Garlic Ginger Red Cabbage

Red cabbage is something most of us enjoy eating when it's placed in front of us, but many of us don't bother to make. But with the Instant Pot to hand, that can all change, and you can have a delicious, Asian-inspired addition to your lunches, rice bowls, main meals and more.

Serves: 6
Cooks: 15 mins

Ingredients:
- 2 Tbsp. olive oil
- 3 cloves garlic, crushed
- 2 tsp. fresh ginger, grated
- 8 cups (800g) red cabbage, shredded
- 1 tsp. salt
- ½ tsp. pepper
- 1/3 cup (80ml) water

Method:
1. Turn your Instant Pot onto sauté and add the oil.
2. Add the garlic and ginger and cook for around a minute, stirring often.
3. Throw in the remaining ingredients and stir.
4. Cover and cook on manual high pressure for five minutes.
5. Do a natural pressure release then open up.
6. Allow to cool completely before dividing between storage containers and popping into the fridge or freezer.
7. Serve however you like!

Vegan Refried Beans

I like to keep a big pot of refried beans in my fridge, so I have a fast, tasty healthy addition to my main meals that feels endless. Remember that refried beans always thicken as they cool, so don't worry. Just add a drop more water when you're ready to serve and enjoy!

Serves: 8
Cooks: 40 mins

Ingredients:
- 1 onion, chopped
- 1 Tbsp. olive oil
- 4 cloves garlic, minced
- 1 jalapeno, minced
- 2 cups (370g) dried pinto beans, rinsed
- 4 cups (940ml) vegetable broth
- 4 cups (940ml) water
- 2 tsp. Mexican oregano
- 1 tsp. ground cumin
- ½ tsp. black pepper
- 1 tsp. salt

Method:
1. Turn your Instant Pot onto sauté and add the oil.
2. Add the onion, garlic and jalapeño and cook for five minutes until the onions start to soften. Stir often.
3. Add the remaining ingredients and stir well.
4. Cover and cook on manual high for 30 minutes.
5. Do a natural pressure release for ten minutes then a quick pressure release.
6. Open up the lid and remove most of the liquid from the pan. Store this in a container.
7. Mash the beans and add some of the reserved water until it reaches a creamy consistency. Be aware that you need them to be slightly runny as they will thicken as they cool.
8. Adjust any seasonings, then pop into storage containers and place into the fridge until needed.
9. Serve and enjoy!

Hawaiian Fried Rice

This fried rice makes an epic meal, so don't be fooled! With the addition of ham, peppers, eggs, soy sauce and pineapple to brown rice, you'll have a filling meal that tastes just wow!

Serves: 6
Cooks: 40 mins

Ingredients:
- 1 Tbsp. olive oil
- 1 small onion, chopped
- 1 red pepper, chopped
- 6 oz. (170g) cooked ham, chopped
- 3 free-range eggs, beaten
- 1 ½ cups (285g) brown rice
- 2 cups (470ml) water
- 2 Tbsp. soy sauce
- 1 cup (225g) chopped pineapple

To serve...
- Chopped scallions for garnish

Method:
1. Turn your Instant Pot onto sauté and add the oil.
2. Add the onion and pepper and cook for five minutes until the onions start to soften. Stir often.
3. Add the ham and beaten eggs and stir well until cooked.
4. Add the remaining ingredients, stir well then cover.
5. Cook on manual high for 24 minutes.
6. Do a natural pressure release for five minutes then do a quick pressure release.
7. Allow to cool completely before dividing between storage containers and popping into the fridge or freezer.
8. On serving day, gently warm in a preheated oven or in the microwave. You can also serve if cold if you like.

Teriyaki Turkey Meatballs

I love making these Teriyaki meatballs on a Sunday so I have plenty to last me through the week ahead! The teriyaki sauce is mouth-wateringly good, the meatballs are tender and delicious and it all works so well when served with a generous serving of rice and plenty of veggies. Yum!

Serves: 4
Cooks: 15 mins

Ingredients:
- 1 lb. (450g) ground turkey meat
- 5 saltine crackers
- 3 Tbsp. buttermilk
- 4 Tbsp. green onion
- 1 tsp. garlic powder
- ½ tsp. kosher salt
- Black pepper, to taste
- 1 Tbsp. canola oil
- 1 Tbsp. sesame seeds

For the Teriyaki Sauce:
- ¾ cup (180ml) low sodium soy sauce
- 1/3 cup (80ml) rice vinegar
- 3 cloves garlic, minced
- 3 tsp. fresh grated ginger
- 3 Tbsp. canola oil
- 4 ½ Tbsp. brown sugar
- ¼ tsp. black pepper
- 1 Tbsp. corn starch

Method:
1. Grab a large bowl and add the turkey, crackers, buttermilk, onions, garlic powder, salt and pepper. Stir well to combine.
2. Shape into 16 meatballs.
3. Take another bowl and combine the sauce ingredients. Stir well.
4. Turn your Instant Pot onto sauté and add the oil.
5. Brown the meatballs for a few minutes on each side.
6. Add the teriyaki sauce, cover and cook on manual high pressure for 10 minutes.

7. Do a natural pressure release for 5 minutes then a quick pressure release.
8. Open the pot and allow to cool completely before dividing between storage containers and popping into the fridge or freezer.
9. On serving day, gently warm in a preheated oven or in the microwave. You can also serve if cold if you like.

Paleo Chop Suey

This Paleo chop suey leaves me speechless. There are so many flavors going on here (fennel- wow!), there's a perfect quantity of veggies and I know that I can throw any meat into the mix and have a wonderful dish ready for me in no time.

Serves: 5
Cooks: 1 hour

Ingredients:

- 1 Tbsp. olive oil
- 1 clove garlic, minced
- 1 red bell pepper, sliced
- 1 cup (75g) mushrooms, sliced
- ½ onion, diced
- 2 stalks celery, diced
- 1 cup (150g) snow peas or sugar snap peas
- 1 ½ tsp. salt, divided
- 1 ¼ tsp. pepper, divided
- 1 cup (235ml) coconut aminos
- 1 tsp. ginger
- ¼ tsp. cinnamon
- ¼ tsp. cloves
- ¼ tsp. fennel
- 2 lb. (940ml) beef stew meat
- 1 Tbsp. tapioca starch
- 1 Tbsp. cold water

To serve...

- Scallions
- 5 cups (1.2kg) cooked rice or cauliflower rice

Method:

1. Turn your Instant Pot onto sauté and add the oil.
2. Add the onion, garlic, bell pepper, mushrooms, celery and snow peas. Season with ½ teaspoon salt and ¼ teaspoon pepper and stir well.
3. Sauté until the vegetables are soft, then remove from the pot.
4. Next place the coconut aminos into the pot, with the ginger, cinnamon, cloves and fennel. Stir well.

63

5. Add the beef and the remaining seasoning then stir again.
6. Cover and cook on manual high pressure for 40 minutes. Do a natural pressure release then open up.
7. Remove the beef (but leave the juices) and turn onto sauté.
8. Mix the tapioca starch with the water in a small bowl and add to the Instant Pot, stirring often until it starts to thicken.
9. Throw the beef and veggies back into the pot and stir well.
10. Allow to cool completely before dividing between storage containers and popping into the fridge or freezer.
11. On serving day, gently warm in a preheated oven or in the microwave. You can also serve if cold if you like. Serve with cauliflower rice or regular rice.

Vegetarian and Vegan

Mixed Bean Chili

Don't be deterred by the long list of spices- this chili is one of the easiest (and cheapest!) out there. Just remember to pre-soak your beans then throw everything into your Instant Pot and you'll have the perfect protein-punch ready in no time at all.

Serves: 6
Cooks: 45 mins

Ingredients:
- 2 oz. (50 g) dried haricot beans
- 2 oz. (50 g) dried chickpeas
- 2 oz. (50 g) dried kidney beans
- 2 oz. (50 g) dried black beans

For the sauce...
- 1 large onion, finely diced
- 3 cloves garlic, minced
- 2 dried bay leaves
- 1 tsp. dried oregano
- 1 tsp. dried thyme
- ½ tsp. ground allspice
- ½ tsp. ground cinnamon
- 1 tsp. chipotle chili powder or paste adjust to heat preference
- ½ tsp. ground cumin
- 1 tsp. smoked paprika dulce or hot as preferred
- 1 x 13.5 oz. (400g) chopped tomatoes
- 1 x 6.7 oz. (200g) sweetcorn

Method:
1. The day before you want to cook, rinse and soak the haricot beans, chickpeas and kidney beans (but NOT the black beans).
2. The next day, drain the beans and place them into the Instant Pot, covered with fresh water.
3. Cover and cook on manual high pressure for 20 minutes.
4. Do a quick pressure release, then drain the beans.
5. Wash and dry the inner pot then set it back inside.

6. Turn onto sauté and add the oil. When hot add the onion, garlic and bay leaf and cook for 5 minutes until beginning to get soft.
7. Add the remaining spices, cook for a further minute then throw in the black beans, sweetcorn, can of tomatoes, plus around 1/3 can volume of water.
8. Cover and cook on manual high pressure for 8 minutes.
9. Do a quick pressure release and stir well.
10. Allow to cool completely before dividing between storage containers and popping into the fridge or freezer.
11. On serving day, gently warm in a preheated oven or in the microwave. You can also serve if cold if you like.

Lentil Bolognaise

You don't have to be vegetarian to enjoy this extra-special lentil bolognaise. As you might notice- it's also oil-free so you can boost the health benefits without compromising on taste. You don't have to add the balsamic vinegar if you don't have any to hand, but it really makes a difference. Top with your favorite cheese or nutritional yeast flakes. Mmmm....

Serves: 4-5
Cooks: 30 mins

Ingredients:

- 1 cup (200g) Beluga black lentils, washed
- 1 x 28 oz. (830g) can fire roasted chopped tomatoes
- 1 yellow onion, diced
- 4 cloves garlic, minced
- 3 medium carrots, diced
- 1 x 6 oz. (180g) can tomato paste
- 4 cups (940ml) water
- 2 Tbsp. Italian seasonings, dry
- Red pepper flakes, to taste
- Salt and pepper

To serve...

- Balsamic vinegar

Method:

1. Open your Instant Pot and throw in all the ingredients. Stir well.
2. Cover and cook on manual high for 15 minutes.
3. Do a natural pressure release for 10 minutes then quick pressure release the rest.
4. Open up and add a drizzle of balsamic vinegar.
5. Allow to cool completely before dividing between storage containers and popping into the fridge or freezer.
6. On serving day, gently warm in a preheated oven or in the microwave. You can also serve if cold if you like.
7. Best enjoyed with freshly-cooked pasta.

Vegan Quinoa Burrito Bowls

Quinoa burrito bowls are a super-easy addition to anyone's diet and they're also brilliant for your health too. Top with as many veggies as you like, plus lashings of chili sauce (if you can bear it!) and you'll have a mouth-watering dish to remember.

Serves: 4
Cooks: 25 mins

Ingredients:
- 1 tsp. extra-virgin olive oil
- ½ red onion, chopped
- 1 bell pepper, chopped
- ½ tsp. salt
- 1 tsp. ground cumin
- 1 cup (190g) quinoa
- 1 cup (260g) prepared salsa
- 1 cup (235ml) water
- 1 ½ cups (255g) cooked black beans

To serve…
- Avocado

Method:
1. Turn your Instant Pot onto sauté and add the oil.
2. Throw in the onions and peppers and cook for five minutes until starting to soften.
3. Add the cumin and salt and cook for a further minute, then turn off pot.
4. Add the quinoa, salsa, water and beans and stir well.
5. Cover and cook on manual low for 12 minutes.
6. Do a natural pressure release, then remove the lid.
7. Fluff the quinoa with a fork.
8. Allow to cool completely before dividing between storage containers and popping into the fridge or freezer.
9. On serving day, gently warm in a preheated oven or in the microwave. You can also serve if cold if you like.

Yellow Split Pea Curry

This yellow split pea curry is probably one of the easiest you could ever make! Just raid your herb and spice rack, throw it all together and leave the Instant Pot to do its work whilst you do something productive. Just double the quantities if you want to make more meals.

Serves: 2
Cooks: 30 mins

Ingredients:

- ½ cup (115g) split yellow peas
- 2 ¼ cups (530ml) vegetable stock
- 1 Tbsp. nutritional yeast
- ¾ tsp. curry
- ½ tsp. Italian herbs
- ½ tsp. cumin
- ½ tsp. onion powder
- ½ tsp. salt
- ¼ tsp. garlic powder
- ¼ tsp. smoked paprika
- ¼ tsp. chili powder

Method:

1. Throw all the ingredients into your Instant Pot, stir well and cover with the lid.
2. Cook on manual high pressure for 15 minutes.
3. Do a natural pressure release.
4. Open carefully and allow to cool completely before dividing between storage containers and popping into the fridge or freezer.
5. On serving day, gently warm in a preheated oven or in the microwave. You can also serve if cold if you like.

Dill, Feta, & Broccoli Frittata

Frittatas make a wonderful meal for any vegetarian, and you can pretty much throw in whatever veggie you like, provided they cook quickly enough. With the addition of feta, broccoli and dill, this one provides just the right touch of saltiness, herbiness and nutrition.

Serves: 4-6
Cooks: 35 mins

Ingredients:
- 6 free-range eggs
- 1/3 cup (50g) feta cheese
- 4 Tbsp. fresh dill
- ½ cup (78g) fresh broccoli florets
- ⅓ cup (80ml) milk or cream
- Salt and pepper, to taste
- 2 cups (470ml) water

To serve...
- Handful of mozzarella

Method:
1. Grab a large bowl and add the eggs, feta, dill, broccoli and milk or cream. Stir well to combine and season to taste.
2. Line a springform pan (that will fit into your Instant Pot) with foil and pour the egg mixture inside.
3. Pour the water inside your Instant Pot and drop in the trivet.
4. Carefully lower the pan onto the trivet then cover.
5. Cook on manual high pressure for 20 minutes.
6. Do a natural pressure release for 10 minutes, then a quick pressure release.
7. Open and allow to cool completely before dividing between storage containers and popping into the fridge or freezer.
8. On serving day, gently warm in a preheated oven or in the microwave. Add the cheese and pop under your broiler for maximum yum! (You can also serve if cold if you like.)

Quinoa Enchilada Casserole

Looking for a meal in a bowl? Want it to be vegan, nourishing and altogeth
Then give this one a whirl. I promise you won't be disappointed. Besides, you u …
enough to feed you for days! Yay!

Serves: 4
Cooks: 30 mins

Ingredients:

- 1 cup (260g) enchilada sauce
- ½ red onion diced
- 1 x 4.3 oz. (127 ml) green chili
- 1 x 11.5 oz. (341 ml) can corn kernels, drained
- 1 x 19 oz. (540 ml) black beans drained & rinsed
- 1 cup (200g) fresh tomatoes, chopped
- 1 tsp. chili powder
- ½ tsp. ground cumin
- ¼ tsp. salt
- 1 cup (190g) uncooked quinoa
- 1 ½ cups (355ml) water

To serve…

- 1 cup (150g) shredded cheese
- Avocado
- Cilantro
- Fresh tomatoes

Method:

1. Simply throw all the ingredients into your Instant Pot and stir well.
2. Cover and cook on manual high pressure for a minute.
3. Do a natural pressure release for 20 minutes, then a quick pressure release.
4. Open and allow to cool completely before dividing between storage containers and popping into the fridge or freezer.
5. On serving day, gently warm in a preheated oven or in the microwave. You can also serve if cold if you like.

Cauliflower Mac and Cheese

Who doesn't love a helping of mac'n'cheese to give them that warm and fuzzy feeling inside?? With the sneaking addition of cauliflower, it gives you all your food groups and still tastes great. If you plan to reheat it, make sure you cook the pasta until it's al dente, otherwise you could end up with a soggy mess!

Serves: 8
Cooks: 30 mins

Ingredients:
- 1 medium/large head cauliflower, grated
- 16 oz. (455g) whole wheat pasta (elbows, shells, rotini, or similar)
- 1 Tbsp. unsalted butter
- 1 tsp. salt
- 2 oz. (55g) reduced-fat cream cheese
- 2 cup (250g) cheese
- 10 oz. (295ml) 2% evaporated milk
- ½ tsp. garlic powder
- ¼ tsp. black pepper
- 3 ½ cups (820ml) water

Method:
1. Open your Instant Pot and throw in the pasta, cauliflower, butter, salt and water. Give it all a good stir to combine.
2. Cover and cook on manual high pressure for 4 minutes.
3. Do a quick pressure release.
4. Open up and add the cream cheese, shredded cheese, evaporated milk, garlic powder and black pepper. Stir well to combine.
5. Allow to cool completely before dividing between storage containers and popping into the fridge or freezer.
6. On serving day, gently warm in a preheated oven or in the microwave. You can also serve if cold if you like.

Chicken and Poultry

Tuscan Chicken Stew

Sure - I could have included this amazing chicken stew in the earlier section, but it's so hearty and well-rounded that I thought it deserved a place all on its own. The fennel seeds make a massive difference to this one, so try hard to include them.

Serves: 6
Cooks: 55 mins

Ingredients:
- 6-8 boneless skinless chicken thighs
- 2 carrots, sliced
- 2 celery ribs, sliced
- 1 onion, diced
- 2 tomatoes, diced
- 2 cloves garlic, minced
- 12 baby potatoes halved (or left whole)
- 1 ¾ cup (415ml) chicken stock
- 2 Tbsp. white wine (optional)
- 1 tsp. fennel seeds crushed with the side of a knife
- ½ tsp. salt
- 1 sprig rosemary

To serve...
- 2 Tbsp. balsamic vinegar
- 1 Tbsp. cornstarch
- 4 Tbsp. water

Method:
1. Open your Instant Pot and add all the ingredients. Stir well to combine.
2. Cover and cook on manual high pressure for 10 minutes.
3. Do a natural pressure release for ten minutes then release the remaining pressure.
4. In a small bowl, combine the cornstarch and water, stir well and throw into the Instant Pot with the balsamic vinegar. Stir well and allow to thicken.
5. Allow to cool completely before dividing between storage containers and popping into the fridge or freezer.
6. On serving day, gently warm in a preheated oven or in the microwave.

Thai Peanut Chicken

Mmmm... until I tried peanuts and chicken together, I never realized that they could taste so good! Then when you go on and add the salty soy sauce and give it a touch of sweetness, you have a chicken meal that can't fail to impress!

Serves: 4
Cooks: 45 mins

Ingredients:
- 2 Tbsp. oil
- 4 onions, sliced
- 8 cloves garlic, crushed
- 4 carrots, sliced
- 2 lb. (900g) sliced mushrooms
- 2 cups (520g) peanut butter
- 1 cup (235ml) soy sauce
- 4 limes
- 4 Tbsp. brown sugar
- ½ tsp. cayenne
- 4 lb. (1.8kg) boneless chicken thighs

To serve...
- Rice
- Peanuts
- 2 lb. (900g) bean sprouts
- Fresh cilantro

Method:
1. Turn your Instant Pot onto sauté and add the oil.
2. Add the onions and garlic and cook for about five minutes until soft.
3. Add the remaining ingredients and stir well.
4. Cover and cook on manual high pressure for 30 minutes.
5. Do a quick pressure release then open up.
6. Allow to cool completely before dividing between storage containers and popping into the fridge or freezer.
7. On serving day, gently warm in a preheated oven or in the microwave.
8. Serve with rice, beansprouts, peanuts and cilantro.

Honey Bourbon Chicken

Honey and chicken are another match made in heaven which you can create with your Instant Pot, whilst saving money and getting super-organized for the week. Yum!

Serves: 4
Cooks: 30 mins

Ingredients:

- 1 ½ lb. (680g) chicken thighs, boneless/skinless
- 1/8 tsp. salt
- 1/8 tsp. black pepper
- ½ cup (75g) diced onion
- ½ cup (120ml) soy sauce
- 4 Tbsp. ketchup
- 2 Tbsp. vegetable oil
- 2 tsp. minced garlic
- ¼ Tbsp. red pepper flakes
- 1 cup (340ml) honey

Method:

1. Open your Instant Pot and add all the ingredients, except the cornstarch and water. Stir well.
2. Cover and cook on manual high for 15 minutes.
3. Do a natural pressure release for five minutes then quick release the rest.
4. Open up the pot and remove the chicken. Dice the chicken and throw back in.
5. Combine the cornstarch and water in a bowl and add to the Instant Pot.
6. Turn back onto sauté and gently heat for a couple of minutes until the mixture thickens.
7. Allow to cool completely before dividing between storage containers and popping into the fridge or freezer.
8. On serving day, gently warm in a preheated oven or in the microwave.

Honey Garlic Chicken

Give yourself another Asian-inspired treat with this honey garlic chicken. It tastes amazing served over rice, makes an epic lunchbox treat and will satisfy even the biggest of appetites.

Serves: 6
Cooks: 45 mins

Ingredients:
- 3 lb. (1.4kg) boneless skinless chicken thighs
- ½ cup (120ml) soy sauce
- 4 Tbsp. raw honey
- 2 Tbsp. fish sauce
- 1 Tbsp. white vinegar
- 1 tsp. sesame oil
- 1 tsp. fresh ginger, grated
- 4 cloves garlic, minced
- 2 green onions, diced

Method:
1. Open your Instant Pot and place the chicken into the bottom.
2. Grab a bowl and combine the remaining ingredients. Pour over the chicken.
3. Cover and cook on manual high for 22 minutes.
4. Do a quick pressure release and open up.
5. Remove the chicken and transfer to a plate. Shred with two forks and throw back into the pot, stirring well.
6. Allow to cool completely before dividing between storage containers and popping into the fridge or freezer.
7. On serving day, gently warm in a preheated oven or in the microwave.

Asian Sesame Chicken

If you're thinking that the Instant Pot seems made for making delicious Asian-meals ahead of time, you'd be absolutely right. This sesame chicken is another to add to your go-to list, bursting with all the sweet and salty flavors you'd expect with a touch of easy meal prep!

Serves: 4
Cooks: 15 mins

Ingredients:
- ½ cup (120ml) water
- ½ cup (110g) ketchup
- 4 Tbsp. soy sauce
- 2 Tbsp. honey
- 2 Tbsp. sesame oil
- 1 tsp. rice wine vinegar
- 1 tsp. minced ginger
- 2 large chicken breasts
- 1 Tbsp. cornstarch
- 3 Tbsp. water

Method:
1. Open the Instant Pot and add all the ingredients except the cornstarch and water.
2. Stir well to combine and cover. Cook on manual high pressure for five minutes.
3. Do a quick pressure release then open up.
4. Grab a small bowl and combine the cornstarch and water. Pour into the Instant Pot, stir well and turn onto sauté until the sauce thickens.
5. Turn off and allow to cool completely before dividing between storage containers and popping into the fridge or freezer.
6. On serving day, gently warm in a preheated oven or in the microwave.

Kung Pao Chicken

There might seem to be a ton of ingredients for this one, but if you have a serious LOVE for Asian food, you'll want to give it a go. Besides, it's not as bad as it looks once you get organized. And if you do, you'll have the most succulent chicken dish, coated in a delicious sweet sticky sauce, boasting creamy cashews and everything you need to give yourself the treat you deserve.

Serves: 6
Cooks: 30 mins

Ingredients:
For the chicken...
- 1 Tbsp. cornstarch
- ¼ tsp. black pepper
- 1/8 tsp. salt
- 1 lb. (450g) boneless chicken
- 3-4 Tbsp. olive oil or avocado oil
- 4 - 6 dried red chili peppers
- 2/3 cup (100g) roasted cashews
- 1 red bell pepper, sliced
- 1 zucchini, sliced
- Sesame seeds and chopped green onions

For the sauce...
- 1/3 cup (80ml) soy sauce
- 1/2 cup (120ml) water
- 2 Tbsp. honey
- 3 Tbsp. hoisin sauce
- 3 garlic cloves
- 1 tsp. grated fresh ginger
- ¼ - ½ tsp. dried red pepper chili flakes
- 2 Tbsp. cornstarch
- 3 Tbsp. water

Method:
1. Grab a large bowl and combine the chicken, cornstarch, salt and pepper. Stir well to coat completely.
2. Find another bowl and add the remaining ingredients. Stir well to combine.

78

3. Open your Instant Pot, turn onto sauté and add the oil. Add the chicken and brown on all sides for 5 minutes or so. Turn off the heat.
4. Add the sauce ingredients to the Instant Pot, top with the remaining ingredients and stir well.
5. Cover with the lid and cook on manual high pressure for 3 minutes.
6. Do a natural pressure release for five minutes then a quick pressure release.
7. Grab a small bowl and combine the cornstarch and water to make a slurry. Add this to the Instant Pot and stir well to combine.
8. Turn onto sauté and cook for a minute or so until the sauce thickens.
9. Open up and allow to cool completely before dividing between storage containers and popping into the fridge or freezer.
10. On serving day, gently warm in a preheated oven or in the microwave.

Greek Chicken Quinoa Bowls

If you've ever wished your vacation in Greece could last forever, check out this healthy, filling and wonderfully easy quinoa bowl. Bursting with the flavors of the Mediterranean, you get olives, you get tomatoes and cucumber, you get beans and you get as much feta cheese as your taste buds can handle. Wow!

Serves: 4
Cooks: 25 mins

Ingredients:
- 1 cup (190g) quinoa
- 1 ½ cups (355 ml) chicken broth
- 1 lb. (450g) boneless chicken breasts,
- 2 tsp. Greek seasoning
- Salt & pepper, to taste

To serve...
- 1 cucumber, chopped
- 1 cup (140ml) grape tomatoes,
- 1 cup (135g) Kalamata olives
- 1 x 14 oz. (400g) garbanzo beans
- ¼ tsp. black pepper
- Feta cheese
- Tzatziki sauce

Method:
1. Open your Instant Pot and add the quinoa, the chicken brown and the chicken. Sprinkle with the Greek seasoning and salt and pepper and stir well.
2. Cover and cook on manual high pressure for 6 minutes.
3. Do a quick pressure release then open and allow to cool completely before dividing between storage containers and popping into the fridge or freezer.
4. On serving day, gently warm in a preheated oven or in the microwave and serve with the suggested toppings, or whatever takes your fancy!

Spicy Italian Faux-Tisserie Chicken

This spicy Italian chicken makes the perfect addition to any lunchbox and tastes wonderful served with rice, sweet potatoes or even some simple pasta. Once you master the recipe, you'll never want to get a pre-roasted chicken again!

Serves: 4
Cooks: 30 mins

Ingredients:

- 4 lb. (1.8kg) whole chicken
- 1 x 26 oz. (800g) can diced tomatoes (not drained)
- 4 cloves garlic, minced
- ½ Tbsp. dried oregano
- ½ Tbsp. dried thyme
- 1 cup (245g) jarred sliced hot banana peppers

Method:

1. Open up your Instant Pot and throw all the ingredients inside. Stir well to combine.
2. Cover with the lid and cook on manual high pressure for 25 minutes.
3. Do a quick pressure release and open up.
4. Allow to cool completely before dividing between storage containers and popping into the fridge or freezer.
5. On serving day, gently warm in a preheated oven or in the microwave.

Spicy Instant Pot Thai Chicken Curry

This has to be one of the easiest Thai chicken recipes in the entire world! You just throw everything together, hit the cook button and leave it to work its magic until you're ready to eat. I really love the way you can throw in any veggies you might have lying around and make it a cheap, filling and awesome meal.

Serves: 4
Cooks: 30 mins

Ingredients:
- 2 boneless skinless chicken breasts (roughly 1 lb.)
- 1 x 13.5 oz. (400g) can coconut milk
- 2 Tbsp. Thai red curry paste
- 3 tablespoons fish sauce
- 1 Tbsp. brown sugar

After cooking...
- 1 Tbsp. lime juice
- 4 cups (700g) vegetables, sliced

Method:
1. Open your Instant Pot and add all the ingredients except the lime juice and sliced vegetables.
2. Stir well, cover and cook on manual high pressure for 8 minutes.
3. Do a quick pressure release, then open and remove the chicken.
4. Turn the Instant Pot back onto sauté and add the lime and veggies. Stir well and cook for 5 minutes until warmed through.
5. Slice the reserved chicken and pop back into the pot. Stir well to combine.
6. Allow to cool completely before dividing between storage containers and popping into the fridge or freezer.
7. On serving day, gently warm in a preheated oven or in the microwave.

Buffalo Chicken Meatballs

This is the kind of meal that they must surely serve in heaven- tender chicken meatballs, plenty of spicy flavor and herbs, and gluten-free quinoa for maximum protein in each bite. If you're not a fan of quinoa, feel free to substitute with regular rice or even cauliflower rice.

Serves: 4
Cooks: 1 hour

Ingredients:
For the meatballs...
- 1 lb. (450g) ground chicken
- 1 large free-range egg
- 1 cup (90g) panko bread crumbs
- 4 Tbsp. finely minced onion
- 2 Tbsp. Frank's Red-Hot Buffalo Sauce
- ½ tsp. garlic powder
- ½ tsp. oregano
- ½ tsp. salt
- ¼ tsp. ground black pepper
- 1 Tbsp. olive oil

For the quinoa...
- 1 cup (190g) uncooked quinoa, rinsed
- 1 ½ cups (355ml) low sodium chicken broth

Method:
1. Grab a large bowl and add the meatball ingredients (except the oil). Stir well to combine then pop into the fridge for half an hour.
2. Form into 24 meatballs.
3. Open your Instant Pot, add the oil and turn on to sauté.
4. Cook the meatballs for 5 minutes or so, turning often until browned on all sides then pop to one side. You might need to cook them in batches.
5. Turn the Instant Pot off and add the broth, a tablespoon or so of Buffalo sauce (opt.), then the quinoa.
6. Top with the meatballs and cover with the lid.
7. Cook on manual high pressure for five minutes.
8. Do a natural pressure release for five minutes then a quick pressure release.

9. Allow to cool completely before dividing between storage containers and popping into the fridge or freezer.
10. On serving day, gently warm in a preheated oven or in the microwave or serve cold.
11. Add veggies and more buffalo sauce if required.

Three-Bean Turkey Chili

It doesn't matter how cold it is outside- with this epic turkey chili you'll be feeling cozy, satisfied and ready for anything! It makes plenty of portions so even a family can have enough to last them for days. And if it's just you, you're very lucky!

Serves: 10
Cooks: 45 mins

Ingredients:

- 1.3 lb. (570g) ground turkey breast
- 1 small onion, chopped
- 1 x 28 oz. (795g) can diced tomatoes, drained
- 1 x 16 oz. (450g) can tomato sauce
- 1 x 4.5 oz. (125g) can chopped chilies
- 1 x 15 oz. (425g) can chickpeas, drained
- 1 x 15.5 oz. (440g) can black beans, drained
- 1 x 15.5 oz. (440g) can small red beans, drained
- 2 Tbsp. chili powder
- 1 tsp. cumin

To serve...

- Chopped red onion
- Chopped fresh cilantro
- Shredded cheddar
- Avocado
- Sour cream

Method:

1. Open your Instant Pot, add the oil and turn onto sauté.
2. Add the onions and turkey and cook through.
3. Add the beans, chilis, chickpeas, tomatoes, tomato sauce, chili powder and cumin and stir well.
4. Cook on manual high pressure for 25 minutes then do a natural pressure release.
5. Allow to cool completely before dividing between storage containers and popping into the fridge or freezer.
6. On serving day, gently warm in a preheated oven or in the microwave.
7. Serve with any of the suggested toppings or select your own!

Beef

Beef Stroganoff

Do you remember eating creamy beef stroganoff when you were a kid? I'd somehow always get dribbles of the stuff running down my chin, but I didn't care because I simply adored the stuff. Now you can recapture those memories whilst taking care of your stomach (and taste buds) all week long!

Serves: 5
Cooks: 25 mins

Ingredients:

- 1 lb. (450g) beef stew meat
- 1 x 10.5 oz. (300ml) can cream of mushroom soup
- 1 onion, chopped
- 1 cup (75g) mushrooms
- 1 Tbsp. minced garlic
- 3 Tbsp. olive oil
- 4 Tbsp. beef broth
- 1/3 cup (80ml) sour cream
- 1 ½ Tbsp. cornstarch
- Salt, to taste

Method:

1. Open up your Instant Pot, turn onto sauté and add the oil.
2. Add the onions and garlic and cook for five minutes until beginning to soften.
3. Add the meat and stir until the browned on all sides.
4. Add the mushrooms and carrots and stir well until combined.
5. Then add the mushroom soup, salt and beef broth and stir well.
6. Cook on manual high pressure for 15 minutes then do a natural pressure release.
7. Grab a small bowl and combine the cornstarch and water. Stir well and throw into the Instant Pot then turn onto sauté mode.
8. Add the cream and stir well and allow the sauce to thicken for a minute or two.
9. Allow to cool completely before dividing between storage containers and popping into the fridge or freezer.
10. On serving day, gently warm on the stove. This stuff tastes amazing over egg noodles or spaghetti. Yum!

Korean Beef Tacos

You just gotta love these fusion Korean tacos which taste even better than they sound! Kimchi, peanuts and spicy mayo with pears, beef and soy sauce? Simply WOW!

Serves: 4
Cooks: 1 hour

Ingredients:
For the Korean beef...
- 1 x 14 oz. (400g) can pears, drained (fresh pears work, too)
- 1 knob of fresh ginger
- 4 cloves garlic
- ½ cup (120ml) soy sauce
- ½ cup (100g) brown sugar
- 1 tsp. sesame oil
- 2 lb. (900g) top sirloin

For the tacos...
- Chopped cilantro
- Chopped peanuts
- Kimchi or coleslaw
- Sriracha mayo or regular mayo
- Flour tortillas

Method:
1. Start by making the sauce. Place the pears, ginger, garlic, soy, sesame oil and brown sugar into a blender and hit that whizz button. Blend until smooth.
2. Next open your Instant Pot and add the meat plus half the sauce.
3. Cover and cook on manual high for 45 minutes.
4. Do a quick pressure release then remove the meat and place onto a plate.
5. Shred with two forks and return to the pot.
6. Allow to cool completely before dividing between storage containers and popping into the fridge or freezer.
7. On serving day, gently warm on the stove before serving with the taco ingredients and enjoying!

Granny's Italian Beef

No, it's not just a name. My grandmother really did make this recipe when she was still alive. And whilst she did teach me how to cook it, it wasn't until I was sorting through her recipe books that I discovered what the secret ingredient had been all that time- pickling spice. Try this one and you'll see! Of course, don't worry if you don't have the picking spice- it tastes just fine without!

Serves: 4-6
Cooks: 1 hour

Ingredients:
- 2 1/3 lb. (1kg) beef roast
- 2 tsp. wine vinegar
- ¼ cups (60ml) water
- 1 1/3 tsp. beef bouillon
- 2 1/3 tsp. minced garlic cloves
- 1/3 tsp. pickling spice
- 2/3 tsp. salt
- 1/8 tsp. black pepper
- 1 whole bay leaf
- 1 x 10.6 oz. (300g) can whole tomatoes

Method:
1. Open the Instant Pot and add the beef, followed by the other ingredients.
2. Stir well to combine then cover and cook on manual high pressure for 35 minutes.
3. Do a natural pressure release for five minutes then a quick pressure release.
4. Remove the bay leaf.
5. Allow to cool completely before dividing between storage containers and popping into the fridge or freezer.
6. On serving day, gently warm on the stove and serve with pasta, big chunks of bread or whatever else you fancy!

Paleo Mongolian Beef

This one is so simple, both in terms of ingredients and cooking effort required, that I'm pretty sure it will become one of your personal favorites. It's best served with rice, noodles, pasta, potatoes, bread (if you're not Paleo, obviously!) or whatever else you can dream up!

Serves: 4
Cooks: 1 hour

Ingredients:
- 1 ½ lb. (680g) sliced flank steak
- 4 Tbsp. arrowroot
- 2 Tbsp. olive oil
- ½ tsp. ginger, peeled and grated
- ¾ cup (180ml) coconut aminos (*or soy sauce if you're not doing Paleo*)
- ¾ cup (255g) honey
- ½ cup (60g) shredded carrots
- ¾ cups (180ml) water
- 1/3 cups (50g) scallions, chopped

Method:
1. First grab a large bowl and add the steak and arrowroot powder. Stir well to combine.
2. Open your Instant Pot and add the olive oil, ginger, aminos, water, honey, carrot and scallions.
3. Stir well then cover.
4. Cook on manual high pressure for 35 minutes.
5. Do a natural pressure release for five minutes then a quick pressure release.
6. Allow to cool completely before dividing between storage containers and popping into the fridge or freezer.
7. On serving day, gently warm on the stove and serve with pasta, big chunks of bread or whatever else you fancy!

Pork

Ranch Pork Chops

These delicious pork chops take ingredients that you probably already have in your pantry and whizz them up to create something that's pretty special. It's a great emergency recipe that works when you're stuck for ideas, you're getting sick and don't want to go to the store, or you're on a particularly tight budget that week.

Serves: 4
Cooks: 30 mins

Ingredients:
- 2 lb. (900g) pork chops, boneless
- 1 oz. (25g) Ranch Dressing Mix
- 1 x 10.5 oz. (300g) cream of chicken soup
- 1 cup (235ml) water (plus extra as required)

Method:
1. Open up your Instant Pot and add all the ingredients. Stir well to combine.
2. Cover and cook on manual high pressure for 15 minutes.
3. Do a natural pressure release for five minutes then a quick pressure release.
4. Allow to cool completely before dividing between storage containers and popping into the fridge or freezer.
5. On serving day, warm through in a preheated oven and enjoy.

Curried Pork Chops

Whoever said that pork chops are boring?? These curry-spiced, sweet and sour, chops with their will impress the toughest judge, and will make a great dinner option for you that's a little out of the ordinary.

Serves: 4
Cooks: 20 mins

Ingredients:
- 1 ¼ lb. (560g) pork chops, boneless
- 2 Tbsp. brown sugar
- 2 tsp. apple cider vinegar
- 2 tsp. soy sauce
- 1 1/3 tsp. curry powder
- 1/8 tsp. ginger
- 1/3 tsp. red pepper flakes
- 1/8 tsp. salt
- 1/8 tsp. black pepper
- 1 x 14 oz. (400g) can pineapple chunks

Method:
1. Grab a large bowl and combine the pineapple and juice with brown sugar, vinegar, soy sauce, curry powder, ginger, red pepper, salt and black pepper. Stir well to combine.
2. Open your Instant Pot and add the pork, then pour the sauce over the top.
3. Cover and cook on manual high pressure for 10 minutes.
4. Do a natural pressure release for five minutes then a quick pressure release.
5. Take a small bowl and combine the cornstarch and water. Stir well then add to the Instant Pot.
6. Turn onto sauté and cook for five minutes until the sauce thickens, stirring often.
7. Allow to cool completely before dividing between storage containers and popping into the fridge or freezer.
8. On serving day, gently warm on the stove.

Pork Sausage & Red Beans

There's something about the Instant Pot that lends itself so perfectly towards comfort foods of all sorts! I love it! This sausage and bean dish is packed with spices and will definitely leave you feeling warmer both inside and out.

Serves: 4
Cooks: 45 mins

Ingredients:
- 1 Tbsp. oil
- 1 lb. (450g) dried red beans
- 1 lb. (450g) smoked link sausage
- 1 large onion
- 5 garlic cloves
- 2 stalks celery
- Creole seasoning, to taste
- 4 bay leaves
- 1 Tbsp. dried thyme
- 2 tsp. dried oregano
- 1 tsp. Tabasco sauce
- ½ tsp. garlic powder
- ½ tsp. ground allspice
- 1 tsp. black pepper
- ¼ tsp. cayenne
- 1 bunch scallions
- 1 bunch Italian parsley
- 2 tsp. salt
- 4 cups (940ml) water

To serve...
- Rice

Method:
1. Open the Instant Pot, add the oil and add the sausage.
2. Cook until brown then remove from the pot.
3. Add the onions to the pot and season with creole seasoning to taste. Cook for around five minutes until cooked.
4. Add the garlic and celery and continue to cook.

5. Add the beans, water, bay leaves, thyme, oregano, Tabasco, garlic, allspice, black pepper and cayenne. Stir well.
6. Add the sausage back into the pan, stir and cover.
7. Cook on manual high pressure for 35 minutes.
8. Do a natural pressure release then carefully open up the pot.
9. Add the salt, scallions and parsley and stir through.
10. Allow to cool completely before dividing between storage containers and popping into the fridge or freezer.
11. On serving day, gently warm on the stove and enjoy. Tastes great with rice.

Caribbean Jerk Pulled Pork

Three cheers for pulled pork! Hip, hip, hooray! hip hip... OK so you get the idea here- I really love pulled pork. And this Caribbean jerk version is right there at the top of my list. I love to make a big batch of this stuff as it's so delicious as part of a meal, makes awesome sandwiches, and it's even great for a quick protein-rich snack when you're fresh from the gym.

Serves: 12
Cooks: 1 hour

Ingredients:

For the pork...
- 3 ½ lb. (680g) boneless pork shoulder
- 2 tsp. brown sugar
- 1 tsp. paprika
- 1 tsp. chili powder
- 1 tsp. garlic powder
- 1 tsp. onion powder
- ½ tsp. salt
- ½ tsp. chives
- ½ tsp. all spice
- ¼ tsp. ground ginger
- ¼ tsp. ground thyme
- ¼ tsp. cayenne pepper
- ¼ tsp. pepper
- 6 oz. (170g) pineapple juice
- ½ cup (120ml) apple cider vinegar
- 12 hamburger buns

For the salsa...
- 1 pineapple, cored, peeled and cut into chunks
- ¼ cup (40g) diced red onion
- 1 jalapeno pepper, seeded and diced
- ¼ cup (12.5g) loosely packed chopped cilantro
- 1 Tbsp. avocado oil

Method:

1. Take a large bowl and add the dried seasonings. Stir well until combined.
2. Add the pork and rub the seasonings into the sides.
3. Place into the bottom of your Instant Pot and add the liquids.
4. Cover and cook on manual high pressure for 50 minutes.
5. Do a natural pressure release then open up.
6. Check that you can easily shred the pork with two forks. If not, return to the Instant pot and cook for additional time.
7. Allow to cool completely before dividing between storage containers and popping into the fridge or freezer.
8. Serve and enjoy!

Instant Pot Carnitas

They're citrussy, they're filling and they're amazing however you want to serve them. I love to pile them high in tacos, with plenty of veggies on the side for a well-rounded meal that touches the nutritional bases and tastes epic!

Serves: 4-6
Cooks: 1 hour 40 mins

Ingredients:
- 3 lb. (1.4kg) boneless pork shoulder
- 1 Tbsp. Mexican seasoning*
- ¾ tsp. sea salt
- Freshly ground black pepper
- Juice of 2 oranges
- Juice of 1 lime (or substitute lemon)
- 1 Tbsp. ghee

Method:
1. Grab a large bowl and add the Mexican seasoning, salt and some black pepper.
2. Stir well then add the pork chunks and stir to coat.
3. Take a jug and combine the citrus juices with enough water to reach one cup (235ml).
4. Pour into the Instant pot, stir and cover.
5. Cook on manual high pressure for 50 minutes.
6. Do a natural pressure release and remove the pork.
7. Place on a plate and shred with two forks then pop back into the pan.
8. Allow the sauce to reduce and when it has almost disappeared, stir through the ghee.
9. Turn off and allow the carnitas to cool completely before dividing between storage containers and popping into the fridge or freezer.

Pork Tenderloin with Soy Ginger Sauce

Easy meat dishes like this are so brilliant when you're meal prepping because they're easy to make, they taste great, and you can easily prep the ingredients, pop them into freezer bags and store them until needed. Try this pork with rice and plenty of Asian veggies.

Serves: 2-4
Cooks: 22 mins

Ingredients:
- 1 x 10 oz. (300g) pork tenderloin
- 1/3 cup (80ml) soy sauce
- 1/3 cup (80ml) water
- ¼ cup (60ml) brown sugar
- 2 Tbsp. ginger finely chopped or grated on a box grater
- 1 clove garlic minced
- 1 Tbsp. sesame oil

After cooking…
- 2 tsp. cornstarch
- 2 Tbsp. water

Method:
1. Place all the ingredients except the pork into your Instant Pot. Stir well.
2. Add the pork and cover.
3. Cook on manual high for five minutes.
4. Do a natural pressure release for seven minutes, then a quick pressure release if needed.
5. Remove from the Instant Pot and set aside.
6. Next take a small bowl and combine the cornstarch with the water and pour into the Instant Pot. Stir well.
7. Turn the Instant Pot onto sauté and allow to thicken.
8. Allow to cool completely before dividing between storage containers and popping into the fridge or freezer.

Fish & Seafood

Shrimp Taco Bowls

This shrimp dish makes a brilliant one-bowl meal at any time of the day and also a great starter when served on its own. To make life easier for you, make sure you collect together as many extras as you fancy whilst it's cooking, then you can simply pile them up when you're done.

Serves: 4
Cooks: 25 mins

Ingredients:
For the shrimp...
- 2 cups (650g) medium shrimp
- 1 Tbsp. olive oil
- 1 clove garlic, minced
- ½ tsp. ground cumin
- ½ tsp. chili powder
- ¼ tsp. onion powder (optional)
- ¼ tsp. kosher salt
- Pinch of cayenne pepper (optional)

To serve...
- 2 cups (370g) cooked brown rice or quinoa
- 1 cup (60g) black beans / chickpeas or lentils, drained and rinsed
- 1 cup (60g) corn, drained and rinsed
- 1 cup (260g) salsa
- ½ cup (60g) shredded cheddar cheese
- 2 Tbsp. cilantro, minced
- 1 lime, cut into 4 slices
- ½ tsp. chili powder
- ¼ tsp. onion powder (optional)
- ¼ tsp. salt

Method:
1. Take a medium bowl and add the olive oil, garlic and seasoning.
2. Add the shrimp and stir well until covered, then cover and pop into the fridge to marinade. Leave for 24 hours.

98

3. Open your Instant Pot, turn onto sauté and add the shrimp mixture. Cook until pink and cooked through.
4. Allow to cool completely.
5. Divide between storage containers, adding the rice, beans, corn, tomatoes, cheese, cilantro and a slice of lime.
6. Pop into the fridge or freezer until needed.
7. Serve and enjoy!

15-Minute Asian Salmon & Garlic Vegetables

Short on time? Want to stay healthy but don't want to opt for plain salad? Check out this fast and tasty salmon recipe. Again, you can just use whatever veggies you have to hand and create a fast meal that you love. Feel free to increase the quantities if you want to prepare even more meals for the weeks ahead.

Serves: 2
Cooks: 15 mins

Ingredients:
For the fish...
- 2 medium salmon fillets
- 1 clove of garlic, finely diced
- 2 tsp. grated ginger
- ¼ long red chili, finely diced
- Sea salt and pepper, to taste
- 2 Tbsp. soy sauce or gluten-free tamari sauce
- 1 tsp. honey
- 1 cup (235ml) water

For the vegetables...
- ½ lb. (200 g) mixed green vegetables (string beans, broccoli, snow peas)
- 1 large carrot, sliced
- 1 clove garlic, diced
- Juice of ½ lime
- 1 Tbsp. tamari sauce
- 1 Tbsp. of olive oil + ½ tsp. sesame oil (optional)

Method:
1. Open your Instant Pot and add the water. Drop the trivet into the bottom.
2. Take a cake tin (that will fit into your Instant Pot) and place the fish fillets inside.
3. Sprinkle with the garlic, ginger, chili and salt and pepper (to taste).
4. Now take a small bowl, add the soy sauce and honey, stir well and pour over the salmon.
5. Place the tin inside the Instant Pot and cover.
6. Cook on manual high pressure for three minutes.
7. Meanwhile, place the veggies into a steamer basket and sprinkle with garlic.
8. Do a quick pressure release and open the lid.

9. Place the steamer basket on the top of the salmon and drizzle with the lime, tamari, olive oil and sesame oil. Sprinkle with salt and pepper, as required.
10. Cover again and cook on manual high pressure for 0 minutes.
11. Do a quick pressure release then remove the steamer basket.
12. Leave everything to cool completely before dividing between storage containers and popping into the fridge or freezer.
13. On serving day, gently warm on the stove.

Asian Salmon

More salmon, but this time it's a chili free zone. Feel free to reduce the ginger and paprika if you're not so keen, and instead add more scallions! Again, increase the quantities as needed.

Serves: 2
Cooks: 10 mins

Ingredients:
- 2 x 6 oz. (170g) salmon fillets
- 1 Tbsp. olive oil
- 1 Tbsp. brown sugar
- 3 Tbsp. coconut aminos
- 2 Tbsp. maple syrup
- 1 tsp. paprika
- ¼ tsp. ginger
- 1 tsp. sesame seeds (optional)
- Fresh scallions

Method:
1. Open the Instant Pot and turn onto sauté. Add the oil and brown sugar and stir well.
2. Add the paprika, ginger, coconut aminos and maple syrup. Stir well.
3. Add the salmon (skin side up), season with salt and pepper and cover.
4. Cook on manual low pressure for two minutes.
5. Do a natural pressure release for five minutes then a quick pressure release.
6. Remove the salmon from the pot and place onto a plate. Cover with the sauce if required.
7. Sprinkle with sesame seeds, parsley or anything else that takes your fancy.
8. Allow to cool completely before dividing between storage containers and popping into the fridge or freezer.

Simple Instant Pot Shrimp

In my opinion, shrimp taste best when done simply in garlicky oil with a touch of wine and a little butter. That's exactly what you get with these babies. Mouth-watering and incredible!

Serves: 4-6
Cooks: 30 mins

Ingredients:

- 2 lb. (900g) shrimp
- 2 Tbsp. oil
- 2 Tbsp. butter
- 1 Tbsp. garlic
- ½ cup (120ml) white wine
- ½ cup (120ml) chicken stock

To serve...

- Pasta or cooked rice
- 1 Tbsp. lemon juice
- Parsley
- Salt & pepper, to taste

Method:

1. Open your Instant Pot, set to sauté and add the oil and butter.
2. Add the garlic and cook for a minute or two.
3. Add the wine and chicken stock and stir well, scraping any browned bits that have stuck to the pan.
4. Throw in the shrimp and cover.
5. Cook on manual high pressure for one minute.
6. Do a natural pressure release for five minutes.
7. Allow to cool completely before dividing between storage containers and popping into the fridge or freezer.

Lemon Pepper Salmon

When you eat a salmon meal like this one, you know you're packing as much nutrition as possible into each bite. Perfect for those who care about their bodies, you'll get antioxidants, protein and plenty of plant-based carbs to keep you feeling energetic and looking great. With a touch of lemon, it's amazing!

Cooks: 15 mins
Serves: 4

Ingredients:
- ¾ cup (180ml) water
- A few sprigs of parsley
- 1 lb. (450ml) salmon filet
- 3 tsp. olive oil
- ¼ tsp. salt
- ½ tsp. pepper
- ½ lemon, sliced
- 1 zucchini, julienned
- 1 red bell pepper, julienned
- 1 carrot, julienned

Method:
1. Open up your Instant Pot and add the water and herbs.
2. Drop in the trivet then place the salmon on top, skin facing down.
3. Drizzle with the olive oil, season with salt and pepper and cover with lemon slices.
4. Close the Instant Pot and cook on the steam setting for three minutes.
5. Do a quick pressure release and carefully remove the lid.
6. Remove the salmon and herbs, and place onto a plate.
7. Throw the veggies into the pot, cover and set to sauté. Cook for a minute or two.
8. Allow everything to cool completely before dividing between storage containers and popping into the fridge or freezer.

Desserts

Very Vanilla Rice Pudding

What's not to like about rice pudding done in the Instant Pot? You can be all sensible about getting the right food groups for your main meal, then just please your taste buds with the desert. Delicious!

Serves: 4 (... ish...or sometimes just one!)
Cooks: 30 minutes

Ingredients:
- ½ cup (100g) Arborio rice
- 2 cups (470ml) milk
- ½ cup (100g) sugar
- 1 cup (235ml) water
- 1 tsp. vanilla extract
- ½ tsp. salt
- 1 free-range egg

Method:
1. Open your Instant Pot and add the rice, milk, sugar, water, vanilla and salt.
2. Stir well then cover.
3. Cook on manual high pressure for 20 minutes.
4. Do a natural pressure release then open up.
5. Take a large bowl and whisk the egg.
6. Add a ladle of rice pudding to the egg and stir well. Add some more and stir again, then pour the mixture into the Instant Pot and stir again.
7. Turn onto sauté and stir, allowing the rice pudding to thicken gorgeously.
8. Allow everything to cool completely before dividing between storage containers and popping into the fridge or freezer.
9. Tastes amazing with a sprinkle of cinnamon and some freshly whipped cream! Yum!

Banana Pecan French Toast

..iazing banana pecan French toast doesn't just smell incredible (trust me, it does!), but with every bite you sink deeper and deeper into dessert heaven. Mmmm...

Serves: 6
Cooks: 45 mins

Ingredients:
- 6 slices French bread, cubed
- 4 bananas, sliced
- 2 Tbsp. brown sugar
- 4 Tbsp. cream cheese
- 3 free-range eggs
- ¼ cup (60ml) milk
- 1 Tbsp. white sugar
- 1 tsp. vanilla extract
- ½ tsp. ground cinnamon
- 2 Tbsp. butter, chilled and sliced
- 4 Tbsp. pecans, chopped
- ¾ cup (180ml) water
- Pure maple syrup (optional)

Method:
1. Find a cake pan that will fit into your Instant Pot and grease well.
2. Add a layer of the bread to the pot then lay a sliced banana over this. Sprinkle with one tablespoon of brown sugar.
3. Place the cream cheese into a bowl and melt in the microwave for 30 seconds or so until soft.
4. Spread the cream cheese over the bananas and bread.
5. Repeat with another layer of bread, then another layer of banana and sugar. This time sprinkle half the pecans over the top.
6. Top with a layer of bread and butter.
7. Next grab a large bowl and beat the eggs with the milk, white sugar, vanilla and cinnamon.
8. Pour this egg mixture over the bread, coating everything nicely.
9. Open your Instant Pot and pour in the water, then drop in the trivet.
10. Place the pan on top, cover and cook on manual high for 25 minutes.
11. Do a quick pressure release and allow everything to cool completely before dividing between storage containers and popping into the fridge or freezer.

Key Lime Pie

Yes, there are a few more steps with this Key Lime Pie than many of the other recipes in this book. But trust me- it will all be worth it in the end. Besides- you'll have a whole desert to last you the whole week, and what could be better than that? Sharing? What's that mean?

Serves: 6
Cooks: 25 mins

Ingredients:
For the crust...
- 1 cup (80g) vanilla cookies
- 4 Tbsp. unsalted butter

For the Key Lime filling...
- 3 egg yolks
- Juice of 8 key limes
- 1 Tbsp. key lime zest
- 2-3 key limes
- 1 x 14 oz. (395 ml) can sweetened condensed milk
- 2 Tbsp. sugar (opt)

For the topping (optional)...
- ½ cup (120ml) heavy cream
- ¼ cup (50g) sugar

Extras...
- 1 cup (235ml) water (for cooking)
- 1 tsp. key lime zest (to garnish)

Method:
1. Grab a 7 inch (17 cm) non-stick springform pan that will fit into your Instant Pot and pop to one side.
2. Place the cookies into a large bowl and smash until forms crumbs. Combine with the melted butter and stir well until combined.
3. Press the mixture into the bottom and sides of the pan then pop into the freezer.
4. Pop the egg yolks and sugar into a bowl then mix on a high speed for around 2 minutes until the yokes turn pale yellow and the mixture thickens.
5. Add the condensed milk, key lime juice and zest, and mix again.
6. Remove the base from the freezer and pour this mixture over the top.

7. Open your Instant Pot and add the water, then drop in the trivet.
8. Carefully place the pie onto the trivet, cover and cook on manual high pressure for 15 minutes.
9. Do a natural pressure release for 10 minutes then release any remaining pressure.
10. Allow to cool completely before popping into the fridge for 3-4 hours to set.
11. Meanwhile, whip the cream with the sugar, pipe on top and decorate with the zest.
12. Divide into required portions and store until needed.

Dulce de Leche Lava Cake

This oozing, sweet and satisfying lava cake certainly ticks all the boxes. It's indulgent and wonderful, but it's also easy, fast and great to pop into your fridge for another hungry day.

Serves: 3
Cooks: 11 mins

Ingredients:
- 1 free-range egg
- 2 egg yolks
- 2 Tbsp. + 2 tsp. flour
- 1 x 13.4 oz. (380ml) can Dulce de Leche
- 1 cup (235ml) water

Method:
1. Take three 10 oz. ramekins and grease with oil, then set to one side.
2. Using a mixer, beat the eggs until thick and fluffy and then add the Dulce de Leche. Beat well until combined.
3. Add the flour and stir well.
4. Open your Instant Pot and add the water, then drop the trivet inside.
5. Cover and cook on manual high pressure for 11 minutes.
6. Do a quick pressure release and carefully remove the cakes from inside.
7. Allow to cool completely before popping into the fridge to store.
8. Reheat by popping in the microwave until warmed though and enjoy!

Oreo Cheesecake

If you've never tasted Oreo cheesecake before, you need to drop whatever you're doing and head to that kitchen. Because Oreo cheesecake is probably the best desert in the entire world! Hopefully this will make six portions, but realistically, it might serve just four.

Serves: 6
Cooks: 1 hour

Ingredients:
For the crust...
- 12 whole Oreo cookies, crushed
- 2 Tbsp. salted butter, melted

For the cheesecake...
- 1 lb. (450g) cream cheese, room temperature
- ½ cup (100g) granulated sugar
- 2 large eggs, room temperature
- 1 Tbsp. all-purpose flour
- ¼ cup (60 ml) heavy cream
- 2 tsp. pure vanilla extract
- 8 whole Oreo cookies, coarsely chopped

For the topping...
- 1 cup (240 ml) whipped cream
- 8 whole Oreo cookies, coarsely chopped
- Chocolate sauce, optional

Extras...
- 1 cup (235ml) water (for cooking)

Method:
1. Grab a 7 inch (17 cm) non-stick springform pan that will fit into your Instant Pot and wrap tightly in foil, then pop to one side.
2. Take a bowl and mix the crushed Oreo cookies with the melted butter. Stir well to combine then press into the bottom of the pan.
3. Pop into the freezer for 15 minutes whilst you prepare the rest.
4. Using a mixer, beat the cream cheese until smooth then add the sugar. Mix well.
5. Add the eggs, one at a time and mix well.
6. Add the chopped Oreo cookies and stir gently until combined.

7. Remove the base from the freezer and pour the cream cheese mixture over the top. Cover with foil.
8. Open the Instant Pot and add the water, then drop in the trivet.
9. Carefully place the pan over the trivet then cover with the lid.
10. Cook on manual high pressure for 35 minutes
11. Do a natural pressure release and remove the cheesecake.
12. Allow to cool completely before topping with whipped cream, chopped Oreos and chocolate sauce.
13. Store in the fridge or freezer until required (if you can resist that long!)

Cinnamon Apples

When you're full of creamy deserts or you have a glut of apples in your garden or at the farmer's market, you'll welcome a light and nutritious alternative, like these cinnamon apples. They make a great breakfast, or a yummy snack when stirred into yoghurt.

Serves: 3
Cooks: 21 mins

Ingredients:
- 3 gala apples, peeled and sliced
- 1 tsp. cinnamon
- 1 tsp. maple syrup
- 3 Tbsp. water

Method:
1. Open your Instant Pot and throw in the apples, cinnamon and maple syrup. Stir well to combine.
2. Add the water and stir.
3. Cover and cook on manual high pressure for 2 minutes.
4. Do a quick pressure release then open the lid.
5. Allow to cool completely before dividing between storage containers and popping into the fridge.

Pumpkin Chocolate Chip Bundt Cake

Whoever thought to combine pumpkin and chocolate chips surely deserves a medal, because this Bundt cake is incredible. It also does a pretty good job of keeping the nutrition as high as possible whilst making hungry tummies of all sizes stay satisfied.

Serves: 12
Cooks: 45 mins

Ingredients:
- ¾ cup (95g) whole wheat flour
- ¾ cup (95g) unbleached flour
- ½ tsp. salt
- 1 tsp. baking soda
- ½ tsp. baking powder
- ¾ tsp. pumpkin pie spice
- ¾ cup (150g) sugar
- 1 medium banana
- 2 Tbsp. canola oil
- ½ cup (120g) 2% Greek yogurt
- 8 oz. pureed pumpkin
- 1 free-range egg
- ½ tsp. pure vanilla extract
- 2/3 cup (115g) semi-sweet chocolate chips
- 1 ½ cups (350ml) water

Method:
1. Take a large bowl and combine the flour, salt, baking soda, baking powder and spice. Mix well then set to one side.
2. Using a mixer, combine the sugar, banana, oil, yoghurt, pumpkin, egg and vanilla in a separate bowl.
3. Pour this into the dry mixture, add the chocolate chips, and stir everything together.
4. Take a Bundt pan that will fit into your Instant Pot and grease well.
5. Pour the cake batter into the pan, cover with paper towels and pop some foil over the top.
6. Open your Instant Pot and add the water, then drop the trivet inside.
7. Carefully place the pan inside, cover and cook on manual high for 35 minutes.

8. Do a natural pressure release for 10 minutes then a quick pressure release.
9. Open and remove the pan from the Instant Pot.
10. Allow to cool completely before storing in an airtight container until ready to be served.

Vegan Pear and Cranberry Cake

Just because you're vegan, that doesn't mean you have to miss out on cake, as you'll see with this soft and light pear and cranberry cake. Feel free to play with the ingredients for this one- I love to add some banana to the wet ingredients and throw in pecans and raisins instead, or even be a bit naughty and go for vegan chocolate chips...the choice is yours!

Serves: 4-6
Cooks: 45 mins

Ingredients:
Dry ingredients...
- 1 ¼ cup (150 g) whole wheat flour
- ½ tsp. ground cardamom
- ½ tsp. baking soda
- ½ tsp. baking powder
- 1/8 tsp. salt

Wet ingredients...
- ½ cup (120ml) plant milk
- 4 Tbsp. sugar or sweetener
- 2 Tbsp. ground flax seeds
- 2 Tbsp. canola oil

Mix-Ins:
- 1 cup (225g) chopped pear
- ½ cup (50g) chopped fresh cranberries

For cooking:
- 1 ½ cups (355 ml) water

Method:
1. Take a Bundt pan that will fit into your Instant Pot and grease well. Pop to one side.
2. Grab a large mixing bowl and add the flour, cardamom, baking powder, baking soda and salt. Stir well.
3. Take another bowl and combine the milk, sugar, flax seed and oil. Stir well to combine.
4. Pour the wet ingredients into the dry ingredients and stir again.
5. Throw in the pear and cranberries and stir again.
6. Pour the cake batter into the cake tin and cover with foil.

7. Open your Instant Pot, add the water and drop in the trivet.
8. Gently place the cake pan into the bottom of your Instant Pot and cover.
9. Cook on manual high pressure for 35 minutes.
10. Do a natural pressure release.
11. Open up, remove the cake and allow to cool completely before storing.

Final words...

When it comes to saving time in the kitchen and sticking to a healthy lifestyle, nothing compares to meal prep. Especially when it involves using such a clever piece of technology- your Instant Pot.

That's why I'd highly recommend that you start implementing everything you've read in this book and start trying your hand at meal prep.

Start small; choose one meal per day and see what magic you can create. You'll be amazed at what happens.

Don't fall into the trap of believing that you need to do it all. You don't need to prep every single piece of food that crosses your lips to be a 'proper' meal prepper. Simply get started. You'll see what a difference it will make to your life.

And most of all, please enjoy the food that you're eating. Treat yourself to delicious food that you can look forward to eating and is also nutritious, easy and fun!

Before I go...

Thanks for grabbing this book! I hope you'll use the info I've gathered here to save yourself a ton of time in the kitchen and eat great food. If you've enjoyed what you've read, please do me the favor of leaving me a quick review on Amazon. It would make such a difference. Happy meal prepping!

Made in the USA
San Bernardino, CA
12 November 2018